WAR IN THE MIDDLE EAST
A REPORTER'S STORY

BLACK SEPTEMBER AND THE YOM KIPPUR WAR

WILBORN HAMPTON

CANDLEWICK PRESS

First paperback edition 2009

The Library of Congress has cataloged the hardcover editon as follows:

Hampton, Wilborn.
War in the Middle East : a reporter's story / Wilborn Hampton.
p.   cm.
ISBN 978-0-7636-2493-4 (hardcover)
1. Middle East—History, Military—20th century—Juvenile literature.
2. Middle East—History, Military—21st century—Juvenile literature.   I. Title.
DS63.1.H3555 2007
956.04—dc22   2006051694

ISBN 978-0-7636-4376-8 (paperback)

2   4   6   8   10   9   7   5   3   1

Printed in the United States of America

This book was typeset in Trump Mediaeval.

Candlewick Press
99 Dover Street
Somerville, Massachusetts 02144

visit us at www.candlewick.com

For

Mary Osborne

and

Amy Ehrlich

In Gratitude

CONTENTS

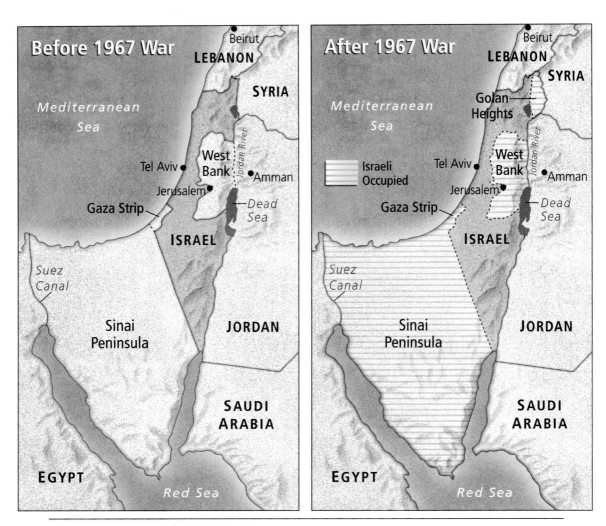

In six days of fighting, Israel captured land from all three of its opponents: the Sinai and the Gaza Strip from Egypt; the West Bank and East Jerusalem from Jordan; and the Golan Heights from Syria.

THE HOLY LAND

OF ALL THE TRAGEDIES the twenty-first century inherited from the twentieth, none is more complicated or poses a greater danger to the rest of the world than that of the Middle East. The origins of the dispute—and the hatreds that fuel it—go back to biblical times, and even today the passions that have led to almost continuous strife for more than half a century have almost as much to do with religion as territorial claims. The stretch of land once known as Canaan, later as Palestine, and now as Israel, is mostly a barren, rocky, hilly, and desert terrain that holds no promise of wealth. But it is a land that all three Western religions—Judaism, Christianity, and Islam—hold sacred, and the zeal with which each stakes claims to it, especially Jerusalem, has kept the region in turmoil.

Any understanding of the Middle East must begin with the premise that no one side is right or wrong. There is no black or white, only a thousand shades of gray.

The conflict that captures today's headlines began early in the twentieth century. Jews from around the world, especially from Russia and Eastern Europe, began immigrating to Palestine, which, like most of the Middle East, had been ruled by Turkey for four

Israel declared its independence and raised the Star of David flag in 1948.

hundred years as part of the Ottoman Empire. During World War I, Britain promised both the Arabs and the Jews its support in creating an independent homeland in Palestine in exchange for their help in fighting the Turks. The pledge to the Jews was in a written statement called the Balfour Declaration. The one to the Arabs was verbal.

After its victory in that war, Britain was given a mandate to govern the region, and for thirty years it delayed fulfilling its promise to either side. Instead, Britain divided the territory in two: to the east it created the country now known as Jordan; to the west it kept control of what was still called Palestine, whose population of Jews and Arabs lived side by side under British rule.

After World War II, there was another mass immigration of European Jews who regarded Palestine as their biblical homeland. They soon began to agitate for Britain to create an independent

Jewish state there, a movement known as Zionism. In the end, Britain turned the question of the future of Palestine over to the new United Nations. A U.N. commission suggested dividing Palestine into two states—one Jewish and one Arab—with Jerusalem as an international zone.

Neither the Jews nor the Arabs were satisfied with that plan, and in the spring of 1948, the Jewish leaders declared an independent Zionist state. Arab Palestinians, most of whom were Muslims, did not want to live under a Jewish government and fought to prevent it. In the ensuing war, the Israeli forces took not only the land assigned them in the U.N. plan but also some that had been designated for the Palestinians. Hundreds of thousands of Palestinian Arabs lost their homes and fled to other countries, mostly Jordan, where they set up refugee camps.

There was strong public support for the Jewish side. After all, Jews had been the victims of one of the most heinous crimes in all history—the Nazi extermination campaign in which some six million people were murdered in Hitler's death camps. In September 1948, Israel was officially recognized as an independent country by the United States and most of the rest of the world.

The Palestinians, especially those who had lost their homes in what was now Israel, began to launch hit-and-run attacks against Israeli settlements of collective farms, called kibbutzes. In 1964 several Palestinian groups banded together to form the Palestine Liberation Organization, or P.L.O. Other Arab nations—led by President Gamal Abdel Nasser of Egypt, which also controlled the Sinai Desert and the Gaza Strip, along with Jordan and Syria, Israel's neighbors to the east and north—became staging areas for these attacks and pledged to support the Palestinians against Israel.

Golda Meir ordered a preemptive attack on Arab forces in 1967.

The confrontation came to a head in 1967. For months, Israel had endured attacks from across its borders with Syria, Jordan, and Egypt, and its Arab neighbors had threatened to invade Israel. President Nasser of Egypt, who championed the Palestinian cause, boasted that the Arab armies would drive the Israelis into the sea and the rivers of the Holy Land would run red with blood.

At the time, Israel was generally considered to be the underdog in the Middle East, a small country surrounded by powerful enemies, outnumbered and outgunned by the Arabs on all sides, the proverbial David against the Arab Goliath.

Finally, Israel decided it had to act. On the morning of June 5, 1967, Israeli prime minister Golda Meir gave the orders that unleashed a preemptive air attack on all three countries. Within hours the Egyptian air force had been destroyed on the ground, and heavy fighting was under way on all three fronts against Syrian, Jordanian, and, in the Negev Desert, Egyptian troops.

Over the next six days, Israel delivered a humiliating defeat to its Arab neighbors, capturing territory from all three countries— driving the Egyptians out of Gaza and the Sinai; seizing all of Jerusalem and the entire West Bank of the Jordan River, which had been under Jordanian control; and capturing the Golan Heights from Syria. In less than a week, the roles of David and Goliath had been reversed.

Yasir Arafat, who was named head of the P.L.O. in 1969, became synonymous with the Palestinian cause.

In the aftermath of that war, new and more violent Palestinian guerrilla groups sprang up, determined to carry on their fight against Israel. In 1969, Nasser appointed a little-known Palestinian named Yasir Arafat as the head of the P.L.O. Arafat, who was the leader of Al Fatah, one of the groups in the organization's umbrella, would remain chairman of the P.L.O. for the next thirty-five years. Until

Outnumbered Israeli tanks fought a fierce battle against Syrian forces for control of the Golan Heights in 1967 and finally drove them into retreat.

his death in 2004, his name, whether hated or admired, would be synonymous with the Palestinian cause.

Because the United States and other Western countries steadfastly supported Israel, the Palestinians came to regard all the world as their enemy, and the more radical groups carried their struggle far from the deserts of the Middle East to cities around the globe to stage hijackings, kidnappings, assassinations, and by the end of the century, suicide bombings and terrorist attacks. One of the most militant groups at that time was the Popular Front for the Liberation of Palestine, known by its initials as the P.F.L.P. Its headquarters were in Amman, the capital of Jordan.

My personal involvement in covering the Middle East began in 1970 and lasted only five years. It included two wars three years apart, each of which in its own way would change the course of the Middle East. But the bloody and sad history of that region was the

A child carrying a tray of food on her head to survivors in the Jordanian town of Kalkilia, which was pounded into rubble during the Six-Day War, in which Israel seized all of the West Bank

one constant story that spanned my entire career as a journalist— whether as a correspondent or as an editor. I can't recall a single week in my forty years of journalism in which there has not been some story from the Middle East, whether it was more shooting, bombing, and killing or some new peace talks or diplomatic maneuvering.

But if the story has been a perennial news item, it also has been one of the most complicated. The heart of the conflict, of course, is Arab against Israeli, or Israeli against Arab. At first glance, it might seem that the Palestinians, who had lost their homes and had their land seized by Israel, have a legitimate claim as the wronged party. Or that Israel, which has been besieged by guerrilla warfare and terrorist attacks since its founding, is more deserving of sympathy. But nothing is that simple in the Middle East.

At the time of the 1967 war, I was working on the foreign news desk in New York at the world headquarters of United Press International, which was then one of two American news agencies—the other being the Associated Press, U.P.I.'s chief rival—that provided news stories from around the world to newspapers and radio and television stations. The following year I was transferred to U.P.I.'s London office, and two years later, I was sent to Rome.

The Middle East kept percolating with occasional attacks by Palestinian groups. Then, in the late summer of 1970, the P.F.L.P. staged one of the most daring guerrilla strikes that had ever been attempted. It ended with a bloody showdown that had Arab fighting Arab in a civil war in Jordan that came to be called Black September.

Nomads driving a caravan of camels in front of hijacked planes at Dawson's Field, a desert airstrip outside of Amman, Jordan

CHAPTER 1

THE HIJACKINGS

SEPTEMBER OF 1970 was a turning point in the Palestinians' fight. In a coordinated action that stunned the world, the P.F.L.P. staged a series of hijackings in which its guerrillas seized three planes. Two of them were flown to Dawson's Field, a disused desert airstrip outside Amman, Jordan. The third plane, a new jumbo 747, landed in Cairo and was blown up as soon as the passengers had disembarked. A fourth hijack attempt, of an El Al Airlines jet, was foiled in flight. A day later, another plane was hijacked to Dawson's Field. By the end, three jetliners were parked in the Jordanian desert with over three hundred passengers being held hostage and the P.F.L.P. demanding the release of some of its members from Israeli jails.

Although hijackings were not uncommon, this was the biggest ever, and I felt a twinge of jealousy that I was not covering it. It was not long before my wish came true. The following day, I had a call from London telling me that I should be on the next plane to Beirut. Gerry Loughran, the U.P.I. bureau chief there, had gone to Amman to cover the story, and I was to go to Beirut to help out.

Beirut at that time was one of the most exotic and beautiful cities in the Mediterranean. It was often called the Paris of the Middle East, and the name was apt. Just as Britain had been given control over Palestine after World War I, France had been given the mandate over Lebanon, and there was still a strong French influence there. Beirut was a vibrant, open city with nightclubs, bars, casinos, and restaurants. Beirut was where the sheiks and emirs of more strictly Muslim Arab countries came to play or seal deals with businessmen from London, Paris, or New York over glasses of champagne at the King George Hotel. It was the city where the spies spied on one another and occasionally even drank together.

As soon as I landed, I went straight to the U.P.I. bureau, which was located in the An-Nahar newspaper building on Hamra Street. The office was in turmoil when I arrived. The hijackers had just released a group of passengers—some women, children, and older people—and Gerry Loughran was giving the details over the phone from Amman. I dropped my bag, sat down at a typewriter, and began writing a story from the notes Gerry was dictating. The other reporters must have guessed who I was because they kept passing me information.

It was only after we got the story filed that we introduced ourselves. The man on the telephone with Gerry was Wadie Hadad, one of the reporters in Beirut. Edmund Hajj, a reporter from Cairo who had been sent to Beirut to help cover the story, had been listening to radio broadcasts in Arabic.

For the next couple of days, I spent most of my waking hours at the Beirut U.P.I. office, writing stories on the information Gerry phoned in from Amman and from what Edmund and Wadie picked up from monitoring the Arabic-language radio newscasts. Then early one morning, before I'd even had my coffee, I had a call at the hotel telling me that Gerry needed a rest and London wanted me to go to Amman to take his place. I had an hour to get to the airport.

Amman, a whitewashed city in the middle of the desert, was a stark contrast to Beirut. If Beirut was wide open, Amman seemed like it was under siege. At first glance, it looked like any other town. There was traffic on the streets, and people went about their business as usual. Then I noticed the men with guns on almost every corner. But these men were Palestinian guerrillas, not Jordanian traffic cops. On the drive into town, my taxi was stopped three times by Palestinians with AK-47s. I left the talking to my driver, and what he said must have been all right, because each time we were waved on.

There was no U.P.I. office in Amman, so I went straight to the InterContinental Hotel, which was the headquarters for some one hundred journalists who were there to cover the hijackings. The first thing I did was locate the hotel's telex machine. Although I

Guerrillas from the Popular Front for the Liberation of Palestine patrolling the streets of Amman

probably would be filing my stories to Beirut by telephone, it is always important to know where the backup is, in case the phones go out. The hotel had one telex, in a small room behind the front desk. Next I found David Zenian, a U.P.I. reporter from the Beirut office who would be translating for me and listening to the Arabic-language broadcasts on the radio.

After checking in, I told Zenian I wanted to see the hijacked planes. He found a cab, and the driver needed no directions on how to get to the airfield. We were stopped twice on our way out of town, and we had to show press credentials to the guerrillas at the roadblock. Finally the taxi driver pulled over and told Zenian that was as far as he could take us. Zenian told him to wait, and we got out of the cab and walked across the sand.

It was a surreal experience. We had just taken a taxi to the middle of nowhere, and now we were heading even farther into the desert into what seemed like a no-man's-land. I had faint visions of the movie *Lawrence of Arabia* when Peter O'Toole is almost dying of thirst and seeing nothing but sand. We climbed to the top of a tall dune, and suddenly there appeared before us, parked on a strip about a hundred yards away, three big jetliners lined up like they were on a tarmac waiting to take off.

A line of Palestinian guerrillas, each armed with an automatic weapon, stood at the bottom of the dune. We just stood there for a while, a group of about twenty journalists on a sand dune looking silently across at three jetliners parked in the desert. We had been there ten minutes, mostly staring at the planes as though they might rev up and start moving toward the end of the runway at any minute, when I noticed off to the right in the distance a caravan of Bedouins, the nomadic people of the desert, approaching on camelback. We all watched as they got closer, then the scene that was about to occur flashed in my mind—Bedouins on camels passing by three jetliners.

As part of the gear I carried, I always had a camera in case I came across a good photo opportunity and there was no U.P.I. photographer around. This was one of those times. I turned and ran back toward the top of the dune. Three or four others must have had the same idea, because a few of us began racing back up the dune. We got there just in time. I snapped half a dozen shots, then the Bedouins and their camels were gone. If the Bedouins even noticed the jetliners or the crowd of reporters, they never showed it.

After another ten minutes or so, we left. It was hard to realize that the three planes had people on board, all of them hostages, sitting there in the heat, where they had been living for several days now, fearful for their lives. The P.F.L.P. had said the aircraft were wired to explosives and would be blown up with the hostages inside if the Jordanian army or anybody else tried to rescue them.

When we got back to the hotel and unpacked, I realized I had forgotten my toothbrush. I called room service and asked for one. A young man appeared at my door almost immediately with two. He told me his name was Ali. He gave me a friendly smile and said he could get me whatever I needed. I had the feeling that if I had asked him to get me a camel, he would have had one in the hotel driveway within minutes.

That afternoon Zenian and I went to the daily briefing at the P.F.L.P. headquarters. There were dozens of newsmen shouting questions in several different languages. The P.F.L.P. spokesman was named Bassam, and through an interpreter he answered them all with the aplomb of a career diplomat. Bassam was a handsome young man with a slightly sardonic grin. He spoke only in Arabic, but I had a hunch he probably spoke English or French as well as any of us.

The one announcement Bassam had that day was that the remaining hostages would be moved from the planes to secret places around Amman. He repeated about two dozen times that all the hostages were being well treated. It gave me an idea.

After everyone else had left, I got Zenian to propose to Bassam that the P.F.L.P. let me interview a group of the hostages. I told him I would be willing to be blindfolded and taken to wherever the hostages were being held. After Zenian translated, Bassam looked at me a long while, then said something in Arabic to David.

Bassam speaking to a group of hostages from the hijacked planes

"He wants to know how much you would be willing to pay," Zenian said.

"Pay?" I asked, genuinely surprised. "Nothing."

Zenian translated, and there was another exchange in Arabic.

"He says two American television networks have already offered five hundred dollars to interview some hostages. Why should he let you do it for free?"

"Because I write for over three thousand newspapers around the world."

He looked at me again briefly, then replied in Arabic. Zenian translated: "He says there will be no interviews with hostages at this time."

But things can change in a hurry on a big story, and the hijackings suddenly became secondary news. After days of being embarrassed by the hijacked planes sitting in the desert, Jordan's King Hussein fired his prime minister and appointed a military government. A dusk-to-dawn curfew was ordered for Amman, and martial law, in which the military takes over running the country, was imposed. The Palestinians responded by calling a general strike, meaning that all shops and businesses would close down in protest. Shortly before dusk, Zenian and I drove over to the P.F.L.P. headquarters.

The sound of muezzins, the criers who call the Muslim faithful to prayers, could be heard from minarets as we stopped in front of the white stone house where the daily briefings had been held. The setting sun was just beginning to tint the blue horizon with a red hue, and the sound of children laughing danced in the evening air.

An armed guard told us in broken English that there was no news conference and we should go away. I looked up and saw

King Hussein of Jordan posing in his military uniform with an automatic weapon only weeks before unleashing his army against Palestinian guerrillas

Bassam sitting in an open window on the second floor of the house. I waved at him. He shouted something to the guard in Arabic and motioned to us to come upstairs.

As we entered the room, Bassam was sitting behind a battered wooden desk, an empty soft drink bottle on top of it. Bassam looked directly at me and spoke in English.

"This is historically a great day for the Palestine revolution," Bassam said. "Hussein has played his last card. There will be a big explosion now. It will be bloody and big, and it will be the last one. There is no other way."

It was clear from what Bassam said that a final showdown between Jordan and the Palestinians was looming. This confrontation had been building for twenty years. At the time of Israel's independence, some 700,000 Palestinians fled or were driven out of areas that became part of Israel. Most went to Jordan—almost doubling the country's population within days—and settled in refugee camps around Amman. Over the years, many of the camps became small towns in themselves with their own schools, police, and services. Yet they remained steeped in poverty, with unpaved streets and only rudimentary utilities, and served as a breeding ground for the discontent that fed the more radical Palestinian groups. Two decades later, most of those Palestinians still lived in camps.

As we left, Bassam smiled, waved, and told us to be careful. On the drive back to the hotel, the effect of the general strike was evident. Dust-caked iron shutters were padlocked on most stores. On one street, a coffee bar was open; on another, a tobacco shop. At one corner, a street vendor sold small round loaves of bread. There

was a line of maybe a dozen people waiting to buy from him, stocking up for whatever might happen.

Several of us ate dinner together that night at the terrace restaurant at the rear of the hotel. Beyond the terrace, there was a sharp drop into a valley where hundreds of makeshift Palestinian houses formed a sort of shantytown. Normally one could hear a buzz of lively noise from the Palestinian camp, radios playing, neighbors shouting to one another, laughter. But that night everything was quiet. There was no sound except for crickets in the garden. All of Amman seemed to be waiting.

Tens of thousands of Palestinians fled to Jordan at the time of the creation of Israel and settled in refugee camps outside Amman.

Smoke from fires caused by almost nonstop shelling billowed over Amman for days during the civil war.

CHAPTER 2

IN THE CROSSFIRE

THE WAR BEGAN at 5:00 a.m. A loud boom that sounded like some-one had set off a cherry bomb inside my hotel room jolted me awake. It was followed by another, and then a succession of sharp cracks split the air like the first day of hunting season. I leaped out of bed and lurched to the sliding-glass door that opened onto a small balcony. The gunfire sounded very close. I crouched down on the floor and crawled over to one side of the door. I pulled back the curtain and peeked out.

Dawn was just breaking, and the night sky was softening into lighter shades of blue. Tracers streaked through the air, their red and white trails lighting up the heavens like Roman candles. Some-where out in the darkness, I heard a rooster crow a new day.

Within a matter of minutes, the gunfire spread all around the city. The spitting rat-a-tat of automatic weapons barked from some-where off to the left, and from the back of the hotel the heavy thud of artillery fire crashed into my consciousness.

In between the mortar rounds and spurts of machine-gun fire, I heard a grinding whir from what sounded like heavy machinery. The noise kept getting louder, and a moment later a line of armored vehicles came into view, moving slowly up the hill in front of the hotel. It was clear by their very presence that the Jordanian army was on the attack. The P.F.L.P. might have a lot of guns, but it didn't have any tanks.

I knew I had to get some kind of story out quickly. I backed away from the balcony door and picked up the telephone. The line was dead. My next thought was of that one telex machine. I tried to roll a sheet of paper into my portable Smith-Corona typewriter on the desk while pulling on my shirt and trousers at the same time. That was hard enough, but a bigger problem was that I didn't have any idea what was going on.

I quickly wrote a couple of paragraphs describing what I had seen from my hotel window. "Heavy fighting broke out at dawn today in Amman. . . ." I began. The editors in New York would add the background. I pulled the paper from my typewriter, wrote the word "BULLETIN" on top with a pencil, and ran toward the stairs to the hotel lobby. Somewhere along the corridor, I heard a baby crying.

Communications in those days were as important as reporting. Journalists in far-flung places often relied on the telex, a landline link that operated like a telephone, except you wrote messages back and forth instead of talking over a receiver. You dialed a number, then typed out what you wanted to say on a keyboard attached to a printer. The receiving party then typed a response. It was sort of like text-messaging over a cell phone.

Zenian was already in the telex room, trying to dial the U.P.I. office in Beirut, but not getting through. I always carried a list of the telex numbers of U.P.I. bureaus around the world, and I told him to try to get New York, London, Rome, or Paris. We finally got through to London.

When I got back upstairs, several of the other journalists had gathered in the hallway. For the next hour or so, we dodged from room to room as the fighting flared first on one side of the hotel and then another. Fires broke out all around the city, sending black columns of smoke rising into the sky.

Among those of us who had rooms fairly close together were William Tuohy of the *Los Angeles Times*, Arnaud de Borchgrave of *Newsweek* magazine, Doug Kiker of NBC News, Charles Murphy of ABC News, and Eric Pace of *The New York Times*. A couple of reporters had binoculars, and we took turns peering across the valley at the back of the hotel or up the street at the front, trying to follow the course of the fighting.

Going outside the hotel was out of the question. The gunfire was constant and on all sides. Even just looking out of the balcony doors proved dangerous. Stray bullets frequently bit chunks of concrete off the balconies, chasing us back into our rooms.

The hotel was on Fahran Street, at the top of a hill. In addition to several foreign embassies that were located nearby, the Jordanian army headquarters was not far away. The entire neighborhood became a battlefield, with the hotel in the crossfire. Jordanian army soldiers had taken positions in a building under construction across the street and were firing mortar over the hotel toward the Palestinian camp in the valley behind it. Once, an army shell slammed into a room down the corridor, leaving a huge hole in the wall. From then on, we rarely approached the balconies except by crawling on our stomachs.

Twice I filed more details on the fighting, but when I went to the telex room a fourth time, the line was dead. In fact, all the electricity in the hotel was off. Tuohy tried the telephone again and got a dial tone, but when he tried calling long distance, it wouldn't go through. The line was open only for local calls in Amman.

Tuohy called the U.S. Embassy, which had its own generator for emergency electricity. The embassy agreed to accept pool dispatches from the American reporters in Amman and send them to our home offices. Pool reports were common in places where communications were difficult or where journalists had limited access to an event. The way it worked was that we would all pool our information and one of us would write a single story that would then be sent to all the newspapers or broadcast networks that were part of the pool.

Since we couldn't file a story, I decided to keep a sort of diary of events. I was in my room typing up some notes when I heard another commotion in the hallway. I ran into the corridor and saw a Swedish television cameraman being carried from his room. He had been hit in the thigh by a bullet while standing on his balcony filming the fighting. Someone produced a first-aid kit and was trying to dress his wound, which was quite bloody. He seemed to be in mild shock.

When I got back to my room, I went into the bathroom to wash my face and discovered there was no running water.

A short time later, an armored car pulled up outside the hotel, escorting an ambulance with a huge red cross painted on its side. The injured cameraman was taken away to a hospital.

About noon, a group of us went downstairs to see if it might be safe to venture outside the hotel and get a firsthand look. The lobby had a huge glass window at the rear that opened onto the large terrace where we had eaten under the stars the night before. I was standing next to a display case that held items one could buy in the

hotel's gift shop. Suddenly the crack of a rifle shot ripped through the window at the rear of the lobby. Almost instantaneously, I felt a sharp pang in the small of my back, but I ran for cover like everybody else.

A few moments later, we all poked our heads out. It had been a solitary shot, probably a sniper from the valley behind the hotel. I went back to where I had been standing and looked at the display case. A spent bullet was sitting on top of it. I pulled out my shirttail and felt where my back was still smarting. When I took my hand away, it had blood on it. I had been grazed in the back by a bullet that apparently had ricocheted off the ceiling. The skin had only barely been broken, but it unnerved me.

Jordanian army artillery units pounded Palestinian camps and guerrilla positions throughout the fighting.

I crept along the side of the lobby to look out the back window, but I could see nothing. Only the hotel cat lay on the terrace, sunning itself, ignoring the war around it.

The more I thought about the incident, the more nervous I got. What if I had been hit in the shoulder? The head? As I considered what might have happened if the bullet had been an inch closer, I noticed that my hands were shaking. I went up to my room to calm down.

As I walked along the corridor, I saw Ali. I asked him if he could possibly get me a whiskey or brandy. I thought a stiff drink might help calm my nerves, but the hotel bar had been locked up when the first shots were fired. He gave me his big smile and disappeared. He returned a few minutes later with a bottle of Scotch tucked inside his jacket.

I started to explain that I only wanted one small drink, not a whole bottle. Besides, the price he was asking was about five times what a bottle of Scotch then cost. But since I had plenty of dinar and nothing else to spend them on for a while, I just paid him.

Ali was very friendly, and I chatted with him for a bit. He told me he lived with his family in a Palestinian camp on the other side of Amman. He had not been able to go home the night before the war started because of the curfew, so he was now stuck at the hotel. He did not know what was happening with his family. The army seemed to be systematically attacking all the Palestinian camps and neighborhoods, and he was worried about his father and mother and brothers and sisters.

After Ali left, I poured myself a finger of the whiskey and drank it in a gulp. Then I went back downstairs to join the other reporters. In the afternoon, gunfire was heavier than it had been in the morning. Tuohy wrote a pool report and was phoning it in to the U.S. Embassy when the line suddenly went dead. Now we were cut off completely—no telex, no telephones, no electricity, no water.

Almost everyone decided to sleep in the hallway that night. I certainly didn't need to be convinced. Occasional bullets were hitting the balconies and even zinging into the rooms. I crawled back into my room, pulled the mattress off the bed, and tugged it into the hall. Exhausted as I was, I still found it difficult to sleep.

The thud, boom, and rattle of gunfire went on into the night, and as I lay on the bare mattress in the hotel hallway, I wondered how many people might be lying dead or wounded out there. During the rush of the day's excitement, I had suppressed any sense of fear that might have crept into my mind. But as I lay on my bed waiting for sleep that night, I thought again how I had been scratched by a bullet in a flash without warning, and how the Swedish TV cameraman had been shot just standing on the balcony. Either of us might have been killed. My thirtieth birthday was coming up in a few days, and I said a little prayer that I might live to see it.

Jordanian army units and armored cars patrolled up and down the street outside the InterContinental Hotel in Amman, shooting at anything that moved.

CHAPTER 3

LIFE IN WARTIME

OVER THE NEXT SEVERAL DAYS, our lives took on a routine. Every morning, the Jordanian army provided a wake-up call at dawn with machine-gun and artillery fire just outside our windows. Then we would all troop down to the lobby to get our daily ration of two liters of water that the hotel was providing from its reserve tanks on the roof. For the rest of the day, we went back and forth between one another's rooms, seeing what action we could with binoculars, then writing up the accounts in case the telephone or telex lines came back up and we could file a story.

But with each passing day, the problems of daily living occupied more and more of our time. Although the hotel had freezers full of food, without electricity it thawed and began to go bad within a couple of days. By the third day of the war, we were eating only two meals a day, mostly from canned or dried goods like pasta or rice. Of course, water was necessary for cooking, and there was the problem of washing dishes and pots.

The lack of water presented another major concern, namely, sanitation. Since there was no water to flush toilets, it was agreed that everyone would use the large restrooms in the hotel's lobby, and the hotel staff would sand them down each day.

In fact, the greatest hardship, apart from the bullets and artillery that were flying around the hotel, was getting by each day on a very limited supply of water. As anyone knows who has experienced a blackout, earthquake, or other natural disaster, you can cope without electricity. But water is vital for basic existence.

The veteran war correspondents had filled their bathtubs when the first shots were fired. But I had been so concerned trying to get a bulletin out, it had not occurred to me to do that. As a result, I had to brush my teeth, shave, and wash myself with little cat baths with only a few cupfuls of water each day, while saving the rest for drinking.

It was amazing to me how life in wartime could become so ordinary so quickly. The only difference was in the details. Like sounds. Rather than the chatter, laughter, and shouts of people going about their daily lives, we heard only the boom, crash, whistle, thud, whine, and ping of gunfire and artillery rounds. Or sights. Instead of the congestion of honking cars on the streets and people bustling along the sidewalks, there was only the procession of armored cars grinding up the avenues, and the only humans we saw were soldiers in battle gear. Or smells. Rather than the aromas of food cooking or fruit at sidewalk stands or even tobacco, there was only the odor of cordite from all the spent ammunition or acrid smoke from the hundreds of fires that had sprung up around the city.

All of this was new to me. Although I had covered the rioting and the entry of British troops in Northern Ireland the year before, this was the first real war I had been in. I quickly learned several things, like how to tell just by the sound the difference between incoming and outgoing artillery. But there was one new sound I could not get used to.

On the second day, the army rolled up a 106-mm recoilless rifle in front of the hotel and began pounding one shell after another down the street. This weapon is badly misnamed. It is not exactly a rifle, but rather a long barrel that looks more like a giant bazooka. It is mounted on a jeep and, far from being recoilless, causes the entire jeep to leap backward several feet with each shot. But the most fearsome aspect of the 106-mm recoilless was the deafening report it gave. Each shot sent waves of percussion with such a mighty force that it shook the hotel every time it was fired, sending glass flying from the windows in our rooms. The noise was so frightening that even the hotel cat finally retreated inside.

We spent most of our days crawling from window to window, trying to follow the course of the fighting. The most frustrating thing about covering a war from inside a hotel is that it is impossible to figure out exactly what is going on. It is like trying to cover a football game from outside the stadium, trying to guess who is winning solely by the cheers of the crowd inside.

It was dark each night by 7:00 p.m., and without lights there was little to do in the evenings. Candles were provided for those who wanted to read or play cards, although it was agreed that they would be lit only in the halls and not carried into rooms since the light from just one candle was enough to draw machine-gun or rifle fire into the hotel.

The hotel laid out beds in the basement for anyone who wanted the extra safety of sleeping there. Most people on our floor decided to stay where we were, although most of us slept on mattresses in the corridor.

Each night, several of us would gather in de Borchgrave's room to listen to the news on the radio and speculate on the course of the war. In the journalistic habit of reducing everything to nicknames, the Jordanian army, whose ranks were made up mostly of Bedouins, became the "Beds," while the Palestinian guerrillas, who were also called the "fedayeen," the old word for Arab commandos who fought against Israel, became the "feds." In our nightly talks, this was a war of the "Beds" versus the "feds."

One afternoon, the hotel manager herded us all into a conference room in the basement. He had received a tip that the Palestinians were going to try to overrun the hotel and take the guests hostage in an effort to bring pressure on King Hussein to stop his attacks on the Palestinian camps. It was while we were in the basement that we met a family that was among the few guests at the hotel who were not journalists. It also explained the mystery of the baby I had heard crying on the first day of the war.

Akbar Khalelli, an Indian diplomat, had just been assigned to the post of chargé d'affaires at the Indian Embassy in Jordan. He had arrived in Amman with his wife and daughter the day before the war broke out. Reihaneh Khalelli, who was only eighteen months old, immediately became the mascot of the press corps. I wondered how the Khalellis were coping. I knew that Tuohy and de Borchgrave, each of whom had filled his bathtub at the start of the war, gave some of their water daily to the Khalelli family. But I worried whether they were getting enough to eat, especially the baby.

After about an hour, we were told the army had secured control of the area, and we all went back to our floors. However, an army unit was now bivouacked in the hotel driveway and on the street outside, which was a dubious blessing. It meant that the hotel was

Yasir Arafat, the P.L.O. leader, met with guerrilla commanders at his headquarters in Amman during the height of the fighting.

at least temporarily secure from Palestinian guerrillas who might have had ideas about taking us as hostages, but it also meant that army soldiers came in and out of the hotel at will, and the lobby became part of their extended campsite.

The Bedouins spoke little or no English, but they were commanded by Jordanian officers, many of whom had trained in Britain and spoke English with British accents. Several times during the next few days, soldiers came in and carted away food from the hotel's kitchen. Once, some of them smashed into a clothing shop on the ground floor of the hotel and carried off armloads of shirts, pants, socks, and underwear.

In addition to the Bedouins, there were some Palestinians in the regular Jordanian army, sons of families who had been in Jordan since its creation. Once, two of them were in the hotel lobby when Eric Rouleau, a reporter for the French newspaper *Le Monde* who was fluent in Arabic, asked them if they were Palestinian. They said they were. Eric asked them why they were fighting the fedayeen, who are also Palestinians. The two soldiers became agitated and said they were fighting the enemies of King Hussein. One reporter who heard the exchange began to take notes. The soldiers suddenly raised their rifles and pointed them at him. They said he was a spy and would be shot.

Fortunately, a Jordanian officer came into the lobby just then. He calmed the soldiers and sent them outside. He told Eric that Jordan was not against the Palestinians but only against their "Marxist" leaders.

Eric asked the lieutenant if he was also Palestinian.

"I am an Arab," he replied tersely, then turned and left.

Eric's question, however, went to the heart of the Palestinian dilemma. At the time of the creation of Jordan, about half of its population were Bedouins and about half were Palestinian Arabs who had lived on the eastern side of the Jordan River. The Palestinian refugees who flooded into Jordan at the time of Israel's independence lived in camps that were set up around the Jordanian capital. The two groups—the Palestinians native to Jordan and the refugees who fled there from what was now Israel—found themselves at odds from the start. The refugee Palestinians agitated for guerrilla warfare to try to get back the homes and lands from which they had been dispossessed. Many of the resident Palestinians, while sympathetic to the cause, now thought of themselves more as Jordanian than Palestinian, and their loyalties were torn in this civil war.

Each day brought glimpses of the death and destruction that were going on around the city. One morning, we were in Tuohy's room taking turns with the binoculars when we saw two men walk outside one of the stone and dirt houses in the Palestinian camp behind the hotel. One of the men had a rifle slung across his back, and the other was smoking a cigarette. The men just stood in the sunshine, looking around and talking.

It was not two minutes before one, two, three, four 75-mm shells boomed across the valley and crashed into a house, kicking up a huge cloud of dust. When it cleared, there was nothing but rubble and a hole in the ground where the house had stood. It was not, however, the house the men had come out of. And the men were nowhere to be seen.

On another occasion, we saw a scene that could have come from an old Keystone Kops movie. Two stretcher bearers emerged from a house carrying a wounded man toward an ambulance that was parked nearby. Suddenly they became caught in a crossfire. The medics dropped the stretcher on the sidewalk and retreated behind a small stone wall for cover. It was maybe five minutes before the shooting died down. All the while, the wounded man lay unmoving on the stretcher and the two medics stayed crouched behind the stone wall. Once it stopped, the two men leaped out, ran to the stretcher, tossed it—and the wounded man—into the back of the ambulance, and sped off.

A Palestinian woman picking her way through the rubble of what had once been an apartment building, destroyed in days of shelling in Amman

CHAPTER 4

No Balm in Gilead

ON THE FIFTH MORNING of the war, word went around that the curfew would be lifted for three hours so that ambulances could reach the wounded, firefighters could fight fires, and civilians who had been confined to their houses for the past four days could buy provisions. Just where they might find provisions to buy was another question.

Several of us decided to take a walk around the neighborhood of the hotel. As we were leaving, I saw Ali in the lobby wearing street clothes. He told me he was going to take advantage of the cease-fire to try to find his family.

A group of us walked up to the British Embassy, which was just at the end of the street. The British ambassador, John Phillips, came out to greet us. He said he had met that morning with King Hussein, who told him the army "cleanup" of Palestinian camps could take several days. The king had also told Phillips that the hostages from the hijacked jetliners were being held in a Palestinian neighborhood. Out of concern for their safety, the army was moving house by house through the area in an effort to avoid full-scale fighting.

As we walked back, a woman ran into the street, waving her arms and screaming. She threw herself at the feet of a group of Bedouin soldiers and frantically began to kiss the dusty boots of one of them. Still on her knees, tears streaming down her face, she clasped her hands as though praying and pleaded with the soldiers not to shoot at her house anymore. An army officer told us she was saying that she had three children and her elderly parents with her and they had no guns and harbored no fedayeen and please don't shoot at her house again. "Don't shoot," she implored. "Please don't shoot."

It was a pathetic sight. I could not watch her anguish for long and turned my eyes away as her entreaties trailed into sobbing. Two soldiers helped her to her feet and half carried her to the hotel driveway, where they turned her over to a man wearing a Red Cross armband.

Dinner that evening consisted of some meat and rice. The bits of meat smelled to me like camel that had died of old age, so I ate only the rice. In de Borchgrave's room that night, Tuohy managed to tune in to the BBC World Service on his long-range radio. The newscaster reported that the fighting had mostly stopped in Amman. We all laughed. Outside our rooms, the gunfire was as savage as it had been on the first day.

The next morning, I awoke again at 5:00 a.m. But instead of the usual sound of mortar fire and artillery explosions, the city was quiet. For the first time since the war began, I heard that rooster crowing in the distance.

With the silence of the guns, however, an even more agonizing sound reached the hotel from the valley below—the screams and cries of wounded men and women, calling for help. The morning

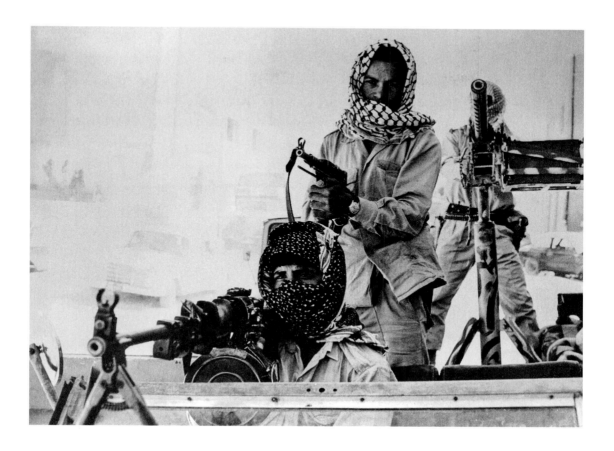

BBC broadcast also brought some disturbing news. The Syrian government had announced that it was sending volunteers to help the Palestinians. The possibility of Syria joining the war on the side of the Palestinians could be disastrous, turning the civil war in Jordan into a broader conflict involving other Arab nations.

Throughout the day, a confusion of sounds told the story of the continuing chaos. There was sporadic gunfire, but the lulls seemed to be longer. Sirens wailed from all sides of the city, and the cries for help that echoed from the valley below mingled with the shrill

Palestinian guerrillas fought running battles against Jordanian army troops through the streets of Amman for control of the capital.

voices on loudspeaker trucks that cruised the streets, calling on the guerrillas to surrender. Evacuees from other hotels kept arriving in armored cars and buses. A Red Cross worker came in and told us that Red Cross planes were making two flights a day from Beirut, bringing in food and medical supplies and returning with wounded civilians.

Shortly before dusk, King Hussein came on the radio to make an announcement. The king began by trying to justify the army's action against the Palestinian guerrillas, who he said had been trying to take over the country. Then he turned to the Syrian threat to send troops to fight on the Palestinians' side. Hussein was scornful, almost taunting the Syrians. "Is this the same Syrian army that fought so bravely against the Israeli invaders on the Golan Heights?" the king mocked, referring to the humiliating rout the Israelis delivered to the Syrians in the 1967 Middle East war.

Then the king announced a cease-fire and said the curfew would be lifted again the next morning. The cooks and the hotel staff, who had been listening to the broadcast in the kitchen, broke into cheering and clapping. They had been trapped in the hotel for nearly a week, and they would be able to leave the next day to try to find their families.

After the news conference, I spotted Ali in the lobby. I was somewhat surprised to see him back at the hotel. I went up to him and asked if his family was all right. He said he had not found them, but neighbors had told him they had all left the first day to stay with relatives outside Amman. I asked him why he had come back to the hotel. He said that it was his job and, besides, he was safer here, either from Jordanian army soldiers who were rounding up Palestinians or from being forced to fight for the fedayeen.

"But tomorrow, if there is a cease-fire, you will be able to go find them," I said.

"Maybe," he replied vaguely.

"But if what the king says is true, the war will be over," I said, thinking that at least that would be welcome news.

"I hope not yet," he said, flashing his broad smile and rubbing his fingers together in the international gesture for money. "War is good business."

In a way, Ali was the personification of the Palestinians' plight. He had told me earlier that his grandfather and father had fled what was now Israel and that their small family farm had been confiscated. Ali himself had been born, gone to school, and lived his entire life in a refugee camp. It was the only world he knew.

Palestinians were known throughout the Middle East as hard workers who would take jobs many other Arabs did not want. They were also known as fiercely independent people who agitated for a political voice wherever they settled. For that reason, other Arab countries limited the number of Palestinian refugees they would accept. For all the sympathy they voiced about the fate of the Palestinians, even their Arab supporters wanted to keep them at arm's length. At his young age, Ali had learned that, as a Palestinian, he was an outcast to the rest of the world—even in the neighboring Arab lands—and he would have to look after himself because no one else was going to.

The following morning, as the sun climbed in the sky and the hour of the cease-fire arrived, scores of men, women, and children appeared on the streets. Warily, edgily, the shell-shocked residents seemed happy just to be standing in the sunshine and listening to the silence. They walked from one house to another, stepping gingerly over the mounds of broken glass and spent bullets to look first at their own houses and then at their neighbors' and survey the damage. A group of children played a game of tag on the sidewalk. A low buzz of human conversation hummed on the streets. A dog barked.

Since the cease-fire seemed to be holding, a group of us decided to take a tour of the neighborhood. There wasn't a house on any block that hadn't been hit, and only a few windows remained unbroken. Gaping, blackened holes yawned in the sides of stone buildings. Cars parked on the street had been smashed into boxes by tanks.

As we walked amid the destruction, laughing children raced along the street, scooping up spent machine-gun cartridges and empty artillery shell casings. The tools of war had become children's playthings.

A saddled horse trotted down one street. No one knew where it had come from or where it was going.

Some of the residents approached us and seemed willing, even eager, to tell us about their experiences. One man stood in front of his house and looked at all the bullet holes in it. He said he and his family had spent the week in the basement. A shopkeeper stood outside his little store that had sold soft drinks, candy, and other food items. Its windows had been smashed and its front door forced open. Inside, it looked like a whirlwind had hit it, and it had been totally looted. Some residents told us stories of army troops going into houses and breaking the fingers of all the men and boys so they couldn't pull the trigger of a gun.

On the way back to the hotel, we took a small detour down a side street. Bedouin soldiers with their faces blackened with charcoal were patrolling the area in groups of twos and threes. They stared at us as though we were Martians who had just landed, not sure whether to be friendly or to shoot us.

As we approached a traffic circle, we saw a group of five soldiers, their rifles pointed at three Palestinian boys probably in their late teens, walking across the street. The boys appeared to be prisoners. The soldiers barely gave us a glance.

I knew in an instant what was about to happen and felt sick to my stomach. I wondered if we should try to do something—find an army officer or show our press credentials and challenge them. Could we stop it? I doubted it. And there was also the possibility they would just line us up with the boys.

The soldiers marched the boys into a one-car garage that stood apart from a two-story house, followed them inside, and shut the door. Then we heard the crack of maybe a dozen rifle shots from inside the garage. The doors opened and only the soldiers emerged.

We walked on.

That afternoon a convoy of three buses, escorted by two armored cars, rolled up in the driveway at the hotel. An officer came in and said they were there to take anyone who wanted to leave Amman to the airport. A Red Cross plane was arriving that afternoon and would take passengers back to Beirut on its return flight. We had fifteen minutes to pack.

I went to my room, threw my clothes into my bag, and grabbed my typewriter. By the time I returned to the lobby, people were already boarding the buses. It was with very mixed emotions that I got onto one of them. I felt like I was leaving a story. But I knew I had to report what had already happened.

As we drove through the streets, we could see smoke from fires all across the city. The convoy moved slowly. At one point, we stopped for an hour because of fighting up ahead of us. By the time we finally reached the airport, the Red Cross plane had already taken off to return to Beirut. An army officer told us another plane would arrive the next morning, so most of us decided to spend the night at the airport and wait for it.

The airport terminal was a shambles. Glass littered the floor. Furniture was overturned and smashed, and bullet holes were everywhere. There were potholes in the runway from mortar shells. Clearly there had been heavy fighting for control of it.

The lunchroom had been ransacked, and there was nothing to eat. There were rumors that the soldiers would search us before letting us leave the next morning and that they might confiscate our stories. I had only one copy of the diary I had been keeping, so I spent the night typing two more copies of it. I put the original in my typewriter case, one copy in one of my shoes, and the other in my underwear.

At first light, we were all outside the terminal, scanning the skies for the Red Cross plane. It was about 8:00 a.m. when we heard the hum of its engines, then watched as the plane dropped out of the sky and bounced along the runway. The plane had brought a cargo of nearly seven tons of food and medical supplies, and some of us formed a human chain to help unload all the boxes. Then we went back for a customs clearance.

I was limping slightly from the folded-up copy of my diary in one shoe, and once, when the copy that I had in my underwear slipped down my leg, I had to reach into my trousers to pull it back up and secure it under my belt. But the Jordanian army officer didn't ask me to open either my bag or typewriter case, let alone to take off my shoes or drop my pants. He checked my name off a list he had, and I boarded the plane.

There were no seats, so we sat on the floor. As we taxied to the end of the runway, I looked out a window and saw a puff of smoke from a mortar shell about fifty yards away. On the flight to Beirut, I recalled the biblical plea of the prophet Jeremiah, uttered during another war for this same stretch of desert that was now called Jordan: "Is there no balm in Gilead? Is there no physician there?"

Palestinian guerrillas blew up the three jetliners they had hijacked to the desert after a final peace agreement was reached in Cairo.

CHAPTER 5

BETWEEN THE WARS

SPORADIC FIGHTING IN AMMAN continued off and on for another two days. President Nasser arranged for peace talks between King Hussein, Arafat, and other Arab leaders to take place in Cairo. Although it was the P.F.L.P. who hijacked the planes that triggered the civil war, it was Arafat, as chairman of the P.L.O., who negotiated the agreement that brought it to an end.

As the talks progressed, the Palestinians released the last of the hostages. The planes were blown up in the desert. The terms of the final peace agreement made clear just how decisively the Palestinians had been defeated. But the news that came later that same day made it almost anticlimactic.

I was at the teletype machine in the U.P.I. office in Beirut typing out a story when Edmund came in from the main newsroom.

"Bill, something big has happened," he said. "Cairo Radio just interrupted its regular program and has started to broadcast readings from the Koran."

I reached down and tore off the tape in the teletype machine and told him to go back and listen. It was only a minute or so later when he came back in.

President Nasser of Egypt, second from right, met with King Hussein of Jordan, far right, Yasir Arafat, second from left, and Colonel Muammar el-Qaddafi of Libya, far left, to arrange a cease-fire in the Black September war.

"Cairo Radio just announced that Nasser is dead," he said, and turned to go back to the radio-monitoring room.

"Get it a second time," I said, but I began to write a bulletin. This was news of such monumental importance I wanted to be doubly sure that Edmund had heard it correctly. It also raised possibilities I didn't want to think about. Had Nasser been assassinated? Had there been a coup in Egypt? It was another minute before Edmund came back.

"They just repeated it," he said. "Nasser is dead."

"Did they say how?"

"Nothing more," he said. "Just President Nasser is dead. Then they go back to reading the Koran."

I hit the send button on the bulletin I had written: "President Gamal Abdel Nasser of Egypt is dead, Cairo Radio reported today." Edmund was joined by Wadie, and they dialed frantically from one Arab radio station to another trying to find more information.

With little hard news apart from the fact of his death to report, I began writing background to the civil war in Jordan, and an old friend and colleague in London, Peter Shaw, who was on duty there, began adding biographical information on Nasser's life and rise to power. Between London and Beirut, we had a full story on the wire within minutes.

My fears that Nasser had been killed proved false. He simply had died of a heart attack shortly after persuading Hussein and Arafat to sign the peace agreement.

Gerry Loughran sent me to Cairo to help cover the funeral. Edmund, Wadie, and I all flew down to join Ray Wilkinson, the U.P.I. Cairo bureau manager, as the focus of the story fractured yet again. What had begun as a triple hijacking had disintegrated into a civil war, and now it was ending with an untimely death that carried an uncertain foreboding.

Whether people loved him, and they were many, or hated him, and they were many, the death of Nasser left a huge gap in the political landscape of the Middle East.

In one piece, I called him "the people's pharaoh." He had been an autocratic ruler, but Egyptians loved him. He was Egypt's George Washington. It was Nasser, as an army officer, who led a coup in 1952 that overthrew the corrupt regime of King Farouk. Four years later, he seized the Suez Canal, the hundred-mile-long waterway that connects the Red Sea and the Mediterranean. It had been built by the French about a century earlier and was later owned by the

British, and Nasser had given it back to the Egyptians. Britain, France, and Israel fought and lost a brief war in 1956 to try to prevent Egypt from taking control of it, but Egypt won.

Nasser was a large man with outsize features who was not afraid to speak his mind. He knew how to play the United States and Soviet Union, the two superpowers in the Cold War, off each other. When the West balked at giving Egypt money to build a dam

Crowds estimated at more than a million mourners turned out to watch the funeral cortege of Gamal Abdel Nasser pass through the streets of Cairo.

on the Nile, Nasser turned to Moscow, and the Soviet Union provided the funds to build one of the world's largest dams at Aswân. For better or worse, Nasser had been the main leader of the Arab world and the most vocal champion of the Palestinian cause.

More than one million Cairenes turned out to watch his funeral cortege pass through the streets. Men, women, and children lined the banks of the Nile and even climbed lampposts and palm trees just to get a glimpse of his casket.

Anwar el-Sadat, a little-known aide to Nasser, succeeded him as president of Egypt.

Nasser was succeeded by Anwar el-Sadat, a former soldier who had been one of two vice presidents under Nasser. But Sadat was so unknown to the outside world that journalists did not even recognize him among the other dignitaries at Nasser's funeral.

After their defeat by the Jordanian army, most of the Palestinian guerrillas who survived went to Lebanon, where they set up camps in the southern part of the country and around Beirut. Newer and more radical groups sprang up. One such group took its name from the civil war in Jordan—Black September.

The next three years saw an increase in Palestinian violence. Their humiliating defeat at the hands of their Arab brothers in Jordan only increased the Palestinians' sense of isolation in the world, and guerrilla groups began to carry out bombings, hijackings, and attacks in any country they regarded as being friendly toward Israel.

One attack that captured the attention of the world was staged by the Black September group at the 1972 Olympic Games in Munich, Germany. Gunmen seized a dormitory where some Israeli athletes who were competing in the Olympics were staying, killed two

A masked Palestinian gunman, top, standing guard outside a dormitory room at the Olympic Village in Munich, Germany, in 1972. At bottom, a member of the Olympic Committee tried to negotiate with the guerrillas, who ended up killing eleven Israeli athletes they had taken hostage.

of them, and took nine more hostages, threatening to kill them as well. After days of fruitless negotiating, German army units stormed the dormitory. All nine of the Israeli athletes were killed by their captors.

If the Munich Olympics massacre captured headlines, other events in the Middle East escaped the notice of many Americans. The United States was being torn apart by the Vietnam War. There was also a presidential election that year.

As the campaign got under way, there was an attempted burglary at a suite of offices in Washington. The police caught the burglars, but the target of the break-in made them investigate more closely. The burglars were caught inside the Democratic Party headquarters, which were located in an apartment complex called Watergate.

For months, Americans focused on a scandal growing around President Nixon, who won reelection, the Watergate burglary, and on the Vietnam peace talks that were being held in Paris. Few noticed during the summer and early fall of 1973 that the Middle East was beginning to heat up again.

Following these U.S. political developments from my home base in Rome, I also noticed stories showing up on the wire from the Middle East about a buildup of Egyptian and Syrian troops and tanks along their respective borders with Israel. There were some reports that the Arabs were planning an attack.

By October, military commanders in Israel were divided over whether there would be war. Some urged the Israeli prime minister, Golda Meir, to order a preemptive strike against the Arabs, just as she had done in 1967.

But this time it was the Arabs who struck first.

Israeli tank units overcame a strong Syrian attack at the beginning of the war to take command of the Golan Heights and advance toward Damascus.

CHAPTER 6

Yom Kippur

ON THE AFTERNOON OF OCTOBER 6, 1973, as most Israelis were observing Yom Kippur—the biblical Day of Atonement on which Jews traditionally fast and pray for forgiveness for their sins of the previous year—a barrage of artillery shells crashed into the concrete bunkers that Israel had built along the Sinai side of the Suez Canal after the peninsula had been captured from Egypt in 1967. At the same time, in a coordinated attack, Syrian warplanes and tanks struck at Israeli positions in the Golan Heights, the upland region along Israel's northern border that it had seized from Syria in the same war.

Although it was a Saturday, I had gone into the office in Rome to finish writing a story. Within minutes of the attacks, bulletins moved on the wire. And minutes after the bulletins, I had a call from London. It was from Richard Growald, the U.P.I. news editor for Europe, the Middle East, and Africa.

"Can you get to Tel Aviv?" Growald asked without even saying hello. "We hear some of the El Al planes caught on the ground in Europe are going to be flown home. See if one of them is in Rome."

"I'll get back to you," I said.

"Find a way to get to Tel Aviv," Growald said. It wasn't a request.

Mike Ross, one of our reporters in Rome, had a good contact at the Israeli Embassy. I asked Mike to see if there was an El Al plane heading to Tel Aviv.

I began to read the first reports on the war. Egypt and Syria, but not Jordan, had attacked Israel, and very heavy fighting was under way. Mike was back in a few minutes.

"They have a plane leaving Paris tomorrow morning and stopping in Rome," Mike said. "They have a few seats reserved for reporters. I put your name down."

I thanked him, although at that moment I wasn't sure just how grateful I felt. In one of the stories I had just read from Cairo, President Sadat had said the Egyptian air force would attack any El Al planes flying to Israel. He accused Israel of using its commercial jetliners as military transport to bring Jews from Europe to fight, and he warned that the Soviet-built Egyptian MiG fighters would shoot them out of the sky.

I went into the office early the following morning to read the latest news before heading for the airport. The Arabs were making gains. The Egyptians had crossed the canal into the Sinai, and Israeli units were retreating into the desert. In the north, the Syrian attack on the Golan Heights stunned the Israelis and put them on the defensive.

The flight took off in the late afternoon. Sadat had been right about the El Al planes. Apart from about a dozen seats that had been reserved for journalists, the jet was full of young French and Italian Jews who were volunteering to help the Israeli war effort, not necessarily as soldiers, but as drivers and in other support operations.

I had a window seat, and throughout the flight I kept looking out to see if any Egyptian MiGs were zeroing in on our plane. The pilot came in so low on his approach to Tel Aviv I could see the whitecaps on the Mediterranean below. Just before landing, he came on the public address system and, like it was any normal flight, gave the local weather and time. Then he added, "The military situation is calm and normal." No Egyptian MiGs appeared.

As we disembarked, a flight attendant stood by the door of the plane and said with a big smile, "You'll have to come back to visit Israel next year . . . and see the Pyramids."

Her joke was indicative of the almost carnival-like atmosphere in Israel. For a nation at war, most Israelis seemed to be reacting with a wink and a smile, assured of ultimate victory with only the time element in doubt. After all, they had won the last war in six days. They figured it would be only days before Egypt and Syria would be part of Israel.

The relaxed attitude extended to the customs officers at the airport, who just waved us all through without inspecting our luggage. Israeli soldiers with Uzi automatic rifles were everywhere, but none stopped us. Outside, taxi drivers were lined up to take passengers to their destinations. I gave mine the address of the U.P.I. bureau.

The driver must have realized I was a journalist because he turned up the volume on his radio and said, "Just a minute, and I'll tell you the latest news." He listened to the Hebrew language newscast as he weaved in and out of traffic, which was difficult because the headlights on all cars had been painted blue because of blackout rules.

"They say they have destroyed all but one or two of the bridges the Egyptians used to cross the canal," he said. "In the Golan, they say the Syrians took some positions in the morning, but our tanks took them back later." He could have been telling me the soccer scores.

The U.P.I. office looked like a military command center. About a dozen people were there, almost all of them on a telephone, talking in loud, urgent voices. I spotted Tom Cheatham, the Tel Aviv bureau manager. Tom was arguing in a polite, calm voice with someone on the other end of the line. Listening to his half of the conversation, I guessed it was the Israeli military censor.

Israel, like most countries during wartime, imposed censorship on what could and could not be reported. All U.P.I. stories had to go through the censor before they could be transmitted. There were certain rules a reporter had to follow. Some were obvious. For one thing, you couldn't report locations or numbers of troops. That was understandable. After all, U.P.I. had client newspapers in Egypt and Syria as well as Israel, and the Israeli military didn't want generals in Cairo or Damascus reading in their morning newspaper what the Israeli army was doing. But there were gray areas of reporting, the strategic importance of which journalists and censors would disagree on. A big part of Tom's job was arguing with the Israeli censors. After he got off the phone, Tom came over. He gave me the keys to a rental car and said he wanted me to go up to the Golan Heights the next day. I was the first reporter from outside to arrive in Tel Aviv, and the heaviest fighting was then on the northern front. Tom wanted me to find whatever action I could and write a color piece—the sight, sound, and smell, in journalistic lingo—on the Golan front. Getting a reporter to the Sinai could wait until more reinforcements arrived.

Tel Aviv was a modern city by Middle Eastern standards,

founded only in 1909. It was Israel's financial center, full of drab office buildings. What it lacked in charm was compensated for by the bustle of business. It was by the sea and reported to have beautiful beaches. But I was not there to go to the beach.

As I drove out of town that Monday morning, Tel Aviv certainly did not seem like a city starting its second full day at war. There were people on the streets, drinking coffee and reading newspapers at outdoor cafés and going about their normal business. But what the Israelis on the streets and we reporters did not know at the time was how disorganized the Israeli defense forces had been at the outset of the war, and how close Israel had come to being overwhelmed in the first hours of fighting.

As it was learned later, on the day before the war had started, despite the buildup of Arab forces on Israel's borders, most of Prime Minister Golda Meir's advisers had believed the Arabs would not attack. At a meeting that Friday, Israel's generals had argued for hours about the Arabs' intentions. Since Yom Kippur started at sundown and would last all day Saturday, the meeting had adjourned until Sunday. The one decision reached was not to call up reservists at that time. Every young man and woman in Israel was required to serve in the military, and they remained in the reserves after their active duty in the event of just such a war.

By dawn on Saturday, Israeli intelligence had confirmed that Egypt and Syria were planning an attack. Even then, some Israeli generals thought it might be a bluff or that the Arabs were planning to stage a one-day raid, not launch a full invasion.

At an emergency meeting, three decisions were reached. Mrs. Meir said there would be no preemptive strike by Israel against Egypt and Syria. If war came, Israel might need help from its friends like the United States, and she did not want it to appear that Israel had started the fighting. It also had been decided to call up some reservists, but not all.

Finally, there had been a suggestion to evacuate to safety all children from Israeli settlements on the Golan Heights sometime that afternoon. It had been Mrs. Meir, herself a grandmother, who ordered that all children be evacuated immediately.

As I drove toward the Golan Heights that Monday morning, two days after the war had begun, there was little traffic, and apart from military trucks loaded with reservists trying to reach their units, there was little to indicate that fighting was raging somewhere nearby. All I had to do was find the war. Driving around the Sea of Galilee, I passed one town where several soldiers had stopped at a café. Some were in uniform, and others were still in civilian clothes. But they were all reservists on their way to report to their units. I decided to follow them. As I got closer to the Golan area, I could hear the boom of artillery and an occasional crackle of machine-gun fire in the distance.

In one small town, there was a sort of rendezvous area with several military trucks and a lot of soldiers waiting to climb aboard them. I stopped. While I was there, more soldiers arrived. There was a school bus full of young men carrying backpacks. Private cars, one a sports model, drove up and parked under some trees. Others arrived in cars that made quick U-turns and sped off. A taxi drove up, and a soldier got out.

Israel had over 200,000 men and women in their reserves, civilians who were being turned into an army. They came by bus, by car, by hitchhiking, even by cab.

I drove on. The roads were by now clogged with military trucks carrying arriving reservists to their units. There was also heavy tank traffic as the machines of war moved from inside the country to the fronts. At one point, I stopped near a village and watched a convoy of tanks grind their way toward the Golan. I asked a soldier who was directing traffic what place it was. He said it was called Rose of Sharon. Reporters are always looking for exotic datelines, and I knew what mine would be for that night's story.

The race to get the reservists and tanks to the Syrian front was more vital than any of us realized at the time. At the start of the war, Israel had 177 tanks on the Golan Heights; the Syrians had about 1,400. Israel had some 200 troops in ten outposts along the forty-mile frontier; Syria had three infantry divisions, about 40,000 men.

The Golan was divided into two fronts—northern and southern. Once it was clear that the attack Saturday afternoon was full-scale war, the Israeli military command had to guess where the brunt of the Syrian attack would be. They chose to throw most of the tanks and men they had available into defending the northern front. They guessed wrong.

Fighting had raged all that Saturday and through the night. Despite a valiant defense by Israel's outmanned and outgunned forces, the Syrians broke through and overran the Israeli defenses. Before daybreak, they had advanced almost all the way to the Jordan River. If they had pressed on, they would have had a clear path into the heart of Israel. But for reasons even the Syrian generals could not explain, the attack halted.

By dawn on the following day, Israel faced the prospect of having to give up the Golan Heights altogether. Moshe Dayan, the Israeli defense minister, flew to the Golan headquarters. The generals

there told him that until reserves arrived, they had nothing left with which to stop the Syrians. Dayan telephoned Tel Aviv and ordered the air force to abandon its plans to strike at Egyptian positions in the Sinai that day and to attack Syrian forces in the Golan instead. To emphasize the urgency of the situation, Dayan told the air force commander, "The Third Temple is in danger." The First Temple, built by Solomon, was destroyed by the Babylonians. The Second Temple was destroyed by the Romans. The Third Temple was the metaphor for modern Israel.

That night, after I returned and wrote my story, Tom said he wanted me to go to the Sinai the following morning. Two other reporters had arrived that day, and he would send one of them to the Golan. I certainly didn't mind the change in assignment. The desert battle would end up being the biggest story. Whatever was happening on the Golan Heights, the battle against Egypt was where the war would be won or lost.

President Sadat, center, in military uniform, studying maps of the fighting in the Sinai with two top Egyptian commanders

CHAPTER 7

THE SINAI

THE SINAI IS ONE OF the most storied deserts in the world. Compared to other great deserts like the Sahara or the Gobi, it is small, covering only about 23,000 square miles. But what it lacks in size is made up for in its biblical history. The 7,500-foot mountain that bears the same name is where Moses received the Ten Commandments. And it was through its sparse wilderness that the Jewish people wandered for forty years as they escaped from Egyptian bondage. The sixty-mile drive from Tel Aviv to the northern Sinai road takes nearly two hours, depending on traffic, and it leads through the Gaza Strip.

I arose before dawn and drove through nearly empty streets toward the highway leading south. The sun had just risen as I approached a kibbutz north of the Gaza Strip. As with many of these farming communities, there was a café and store that sold produce from its fields. I stopped to have coffee.

Two young women were on duty. The one who served me had an American accent, and I asked her where she was from. Her name was Sarah, and she was a college student from Chicago. She had come to Israel that summer to work on a kibbutz and had decided to stay. She was not too worried about the war, although it was now the harvest season, and all the men had left to join the army, leaving them shorthanded in the fields.

As I approached Gaza, I began to feel a bit uneasy. The narrow strip of land that lies along the Mediterranean Sea was the home of more than half a million people, mostly Palestinians. Until six years earlier, Gaza had been under Egyptian control, but Israel had seized it in the 1967 war and would keep it for nearly forty more years, later even building houses and Jewish settlements there.

At that time, the local Arab population was known to be openly hostile to foreigners, sometimes throwing rocks at cars driving through. As I entered Gaza City, it was still early morning, and there were not many people about. There were a few women doing early shopping at the markets, and some men sat at outdoor cafés, reading newspapers and drinking coffee. A group of school-age children played along the dusty road, kicking a rock like a soccer ball. They all stopped and stared at the rental car that drove by, but no one pulled a gun or picked up a stone.

The sun was well up in the sky by the time I turned onto the northern Sinai road at El Arish, a paradise of an oasis with groves of palm trees and an expanse of the whitest sand I had ever seen. From my car I could see the blue waters of the Mediterranean just off to my right. It was not long before the scenery changed.

My assignment was the same as it had been on the Golan Heights—to find some action, then return to Tel Aviv and write my story. The daily U.P.I. news package would have the main war story and a color sidebar from each of the two fronts—Syria in the north and Egypt in the south—plus whatever other sidebar stories the other reporters found. I was completely free to go wherever I wanted, as long as I got a better story from the Sinai than the A.P. My plan was to drive as far as I could on the Sinai road, taking notes and stopping to talk to any groups of soldiers I might see.

At times, the desert road resembled a freeway at rush hour. Long lines of tanks, armored cars, artillery vehicles, and jeeps often clogged the road bumper-to-bumper. Then there were stretches of open highway that were like a rural road. The only constant was that nearly all the traffic was heading west, toward the Suez Canal. Only occasionally did I see any kind of vehicle driving east, and it was nearly always an empty military truck, troop carrier, or bus that, having delivered its cargo of soldiers or supplies to the front, was going back to pick up more.

Once, I met a convoy of three trucks that had just pulled onto the road and was heading back toward Tel Aviv. All three were piled with radio equipment, filing cabinets, and cardboard boxes, and they had blue United Nations flags flapping from their antennas.

The scenery was no less incongruous. All along the way, the beautiful undulating oceans of desert sand were dotted with rusted tanks, trucks, and jeeps that had been left there from the previous war six years earlier. Some were Egyptian, some Israeli.

At one point the traffic slowed to a crawl, and it was clear that something just ahead was tying it up. Every so often a vehicle would pull out and pass whatever was slowing us down. As I got closer, I could see that some huge machine was poking along at about two miles per hour, like a tractor puttering down on a narrow country road.

Although there were few cars coming east, the vehicle was so long that the jeeps and tanks had to wait until the road was well clear to pass it. When it came my turn, I nosed my car out into the other lane and passed it as fast as I could. It was one of the longest vehicles I had ever seen. It was only when I was about halfway around it that I realized what it was. It was a pontoon bridge–building machine.

I knew I had my story for the day. The Israelis were planning to cross the canal and invade Egypt proper. They certainly wouldn't be bringing in these huge machines that could lay down a bridge in a

Pontoon bridges were moved into the desert at the start of the war.

couple of hours if they didn't plan on using them. After I got past the machine, I drove onto a hard spot on the side of the road and stopped. I wanted pictures to go with my story. As the giant behemoth clanked by, I took several shots.

Although I didn't realize it then, any plan for Israel to bridge the Suez Canal into Egypt was mostly wishful thinking. As a postwar inquiry discovered, Israeli forces in the Sinai, just as they had been on the Syrian front, had been shocked by the Egyptian attack. In the first minutes of the war, Egyptian gunners rained some 10,000 artillery rounds on Israeli positions. Fifteen minutes later, a wave of 4,000 Egyptian troops piled into 720 boats to cross the canal. The Egyptians then brought up their own bridge-building machines, and by midnight of the first day, eight bridges strong enough to hold tanks had been laid across the waterway. Within twenty-four hours of the first shot being fired, Egypt had 100,000 soldiers in the Sinai, along with over 1,000 tanks. Israel was on its heels.

For the first time in its existence, Israel was being forced to fight defensive rather than offensive battles. The surprise attacks seemed to have paralyzed the Israeli generals, who for two days clung stubbornly to their original battle plan despite the fact that their forces were being driven back farther into the desert and they were outnumbered five to one.

The full extent of the Egyptian gains in the desert was unknown as I drove across the Sinai that morning. As I got closer to the front, the number of checkpoints increased. The first two or three had been almost perfunctory—a couple of soldiers beside a jeep, who just waved me on when I said "journalist." But the soldiers at the last one had been more inquisitive, asking me my name, my news organization, where I was from.

Within minutes of the initial bombardment, a force of 4,000 Egyptian commandos began to cross the Suez Canal in rubber and wooden boats, some even rowing their way across.

Now the scenery changed again. Every hundred yards or so, an Israeli tank crew was parked off the road in the desert, taking a break from the fighting or waiting for orders to join it. Some sat beside their tanks, resting in the shade of their tracks. Others were stretched out in the sand, their shirts open, sunbathing. I passed one lone tank just beside the road, on which a single soldier sat on a stool under an umbrella with a small Star of David flag attached to the top. He was reading a book.

It was not much farther before I ran into another roadblock. A lieutenant was standing by a jeep parked in the middle of the road. Two tanks were off in the sand, their hatches open. A soldier stood in each, helmet on, holding a two-way radio. The lieutenant seemed surprised to find a civilian journalist in a rental car at his checkpoint. "This is a war zone," he said. "There are Egyptians out there. You could get killed."

I countered by asking him how many Egyptians there were. Where were they? How was the fighting going? Had Israel taken back any of the territory it had lost at the beginning of the war? He seemed amused that I would be asking such questions.

Just then, the radio in his jeep crackled, and he went to answer it. I looked back at the tanks. The two soldiers had disappeared inside them and shut the hatches.

As I stood there waiting to see what happened, three Israeli jets suddenly screamed up from behind me, flying very low, and disappeared over the horizon. I decided I had seen enough action and got back in my car and headed east. While I was certain neither the Israeli jets nor the Egyptian tanks they were chasing would fire at my rental car, there seemed no sense in tempting fate that a stray shell might land nearby.

I had driven only a short distance when I saw, on the crest of a dune about a hundred yards off the road, a caravan of five camels, led by an Arab in flowing robes, crossing the desert. Oblivious to jet fighters streaking through the skies or tanks invading his turf, the nomad was herding his camels across the Sinai. I thought of the camel driver who had wandered across another desert in front of the hijacked planes in Jordan three years earlier. It was almost a comfort to see the nomad's disregard for the foreigners who were fighting their war in his backyard.

On the way back to Tel Aviv, I drove by the old United Nations outpost, now completely abandoned and deserted. At El Arish, I

The Israeli air force again played a crucial role in the fighting, as flights of warplanes established dominance in the skies over the Sinai despite Egypt's use of SAM-6 missiles.

passed a group of Arab schoolchildren walking home from the day's classes. They were laughing and talking among themselves and seemed not to even notice the long trail of weapons and soldiers on the road.

It was already dusk by the time I got to the U.P.I. bureau. I wrote my story, leading with the fact that Israel was moving bridge-building machines toward the Suez Canal with the apparent intention of invading Egypt. No sooner had the first paragraph cleared the wire than the telephone rang. It was the Israeli censor telling Tom we could not transmit the story. Tom argued that the machine had been on the main Sinai highway and we had pictures of it. The censor said we couldn't transmit the pictures either.

It seemed unfair. The Egyptians had reconnaissance flights crossing the Sinai all day, and they would surely have seen that huge machine lumbering across the desert. But there was no arguing with the censor. I returned to the hotel rather depressed. My job was to find the real story of what was happening out in the desert, and I was fairly certain I had this one all to myself. No reporter likes to have a genuine scoop stolen by censorship.

Long-range Israeli artillery bombarded Syrian positions on the Golan Heights.

CHAPTER 8

PLAYING CAT AND MOUSE

THE NEXT DAY, I again arose before dawn and drove south. The drive through Gaza was even less eventful than on the previous day. My rental car didn't even attract curious glances. Shortly after the turnoff at El Arish, however, the traffic picked up.

For the next several miles, it was like driving past a chain of strip malls that offered nothing but military hardware. The sides of the road were dotted with bivouac areas at which jeeps, tanks, and trucks were parked. At one camp, under a clump of palm trees, a group of Israeli soldiers were cutting off branches to build makeshift Sukkoth tabernacles for the annual fall harvest celebration that would begin the following day.

The Feast of Tabernacles, as Sukkoth is also called, comes five days after Yom Kippur and lasts for a week. During that time, observant Jews take their meals under covered tabernacles to recall the shelters of the Jews during their period of wandering in the wilderness of this very same Sinai after their flight from Egypt.

I passed one large bivouac area where a dozen or more large tents had been set up and scores of soldiers were milling about. I decided to try to talk to some. On one side of the area, two water

The war was fought during the Jewish holy days, and many Israeli soldiers, like this one in the Sinai, put on prayer shawls for morning prayers before the day's battle.

tanks had been set up with a pipe leading straight down. A line of soldiers stood naked at each, waiting their turns at the improvised shower. Each soldier got two squirts of water—one to soap himself and a second a few moments later to rinse off.

A truck drove up with a dozen or so soldiers in the back, their faces streaked with mud and dirt. It was clear they had just returned from the front. I went over to them and found one officer, a lieutenant who would not give his name but was willing to talk a bit.

"It is going all right," he said when I asked him about the fighting. "We will win. Another three or four days. Maybe." He did not smile, however, and his estimate of how long it would take Israel to win was more like a question than a statement.

Back on the road, I had gone only a couple of miles when I saw two more rental cars parked beside the road, their occupants standing beside them. As I got closer, I saw that one of them was Bill Tuohy. I pulled over. A CBS correspondent and his cameraman were in the other car. Tuohy said they had been driving west when they had heard artillery fire. We saw nothing, however, and drove on, now a caravan of three cars.

A short distance later, we came up behind a tank moving slowly down the road, a jeep in front of it with four soldiers inside. We crept along behind the tank, driving maybe five miles per hour. We must have made a comical sight for any reconnaissance planes flying overhead—a jeep, followed by a tank, followed by three rental cars.

My car was directly behind the tank. Two soldiers stood in the top of it, the turret of which turned first right and then left, scanning the desert for Egyptian tanks. The four men in the jeep were spotters. They wore huge goggles and earphones.

Suddenly, the two tank crew members dropped down inside and slammed the hatch shut. The tank swerved off the road, churning up a cloud of sand as it moved into high gear and lit out into the desert. We got out of our cars to watch. There was a small dune just to the right of the road, and we climbed it to get a better view. There were three Egyptian tanks just a couple of hundred yards into the desert that had been zeroing in on one Israeli tank, and the tank we had been following was racing to help.

As we watched this desert dogfight through binoculars, the shrill whistle of an incoming Egyptian rocket pierced our ears. We all threw ourselves facedown into the dune. It exploded not that far off, and we all agreed it was time to leave. As we walked back toward the cars, dusting sand from our clothes, another scream splintered the sky.

A flight of Israeli jets, flying so low I thought they would slam into a good-size dune if it suddenly rose up in front of them, shot past us, then banked and turned back on the far horizon. The Israeli spotters had apparently called in air support, and the planes were thundering to the rescue like the cavalry in an old Western movie.

There were five planes in the flight, and as they came back for their second pass, this time with the Egyptian tanks in their gun sights, they climbed very high in the sky. Then one after the other swooped low again, like giant birds diving for prey. One, two, three, four rose to dizzying heights, then plummeted to earth, pulling out of their dives just above the desert and zooming in low on their targets.

Then, silently, swiftly, without warning, a puff of smoke and a flash of fire hit the fifth plane. It began to spiral toward the earth and crashed into the desert just out of our view. We kept searching the sky for parachutes. There were none to be seen.

An Egyptian SAM-6, the deadly surface-to-air missile that was the latest in the Soviet arsenal at that time, apparently had locked in on the Israeli jets in time to get the last one as it prepared to make its attack.

Old Soviet-built missiles seized by the Israelis in Egypt

A captured Egyptian SAM-6 missile being escorted across the Sinai by an Israeli tank

We all sprinted to our cars, made U-turns, and headed east. I kept an old-fashioned clipboard in the front passenger seat of the car, and as I drove I began writing my story in longhand while it was still fresh in my mind. Since there were no telephones for me to use in the desert, I had to wait until I got back to Tel Aviv to write my story. But if I could get most of it on paper while I was driving, all I had to do was type it out when I got to the bureau. Getting my story out on the wire quickly was an important factor. Newspaper editors often took the first story that came in—whether it was U.P.I. or A.P.—and published it rather than waiting to compare which agency had the better one.

Once again, I was thwarted by the censor. He would not clear my account of the plane being shot down. It seemed arbitrary to me. Even the Israeli military was reporting that it had lost planes to Egyptian fire, but the censor would not let me report that one had been shot down by a SAM. He cleared the rest of my story about the tank battle.

The tank had been the mainstay of both the Israeli and Arab armies, but this war was seeing the tank's reputation of invincibility challenged. Egyptian foot soldiers were armed with a new missile called the Sagger, which had a range of 3,000 yards and could knock out a tank with a single shot. But on this day, war in the desert was mostly still a tank's battle. The Israelis and Egyptians were playing a deadly cat-and-mouse game in the Sinai, although it was often difficult to tell who was the cat and who was the mouse.

There was an unwelcome surprise the next morning. Because there were now so many reporters traveling to and from the two fronts, the Israeli military wanted an officer to accompany each car of reporters driving to and from the war zones. I told Tom that I was unhappy with that arrangement, but he wanted to make an effort to accommodate the military, so I said I would try it. He also wanted a U.P.I. photographer to go with me.

There is a long history of reporters traveling with military units in wartime. During World War II, Korea, and Vietnam, for example, journalists often had to depend on the army they were covering for transportation to the front as well as for food, lodging, and security. And early in the new century, there was the issue of reporters being "embedded" with the military in Iraq. There was always some debate about whether a reporter who depended on a certain company of soldiers for transport, food, and safety could still be objective. But I always felt that a good reporter would write what he or she saw and heard no matter who provided the rides and meals.

Although the Israeli military said the placement of officers in reporters' cars was for security, it seemed clear to me that they wanted to keep an eye on the journalists. And I wasn't sure that having an Israeli soldier in the car wouldn't just make it more of a target.

We were assigned an Israeli major named Shlomo. There were problems from the start. For one thing, Major Shlomo wanted to carry a rifle in the car. I refused. The major insisted. If the rifle didn't go, he didn't go. I said that was fine with me. Then I recalled Tom wanted to try this arrangement, so we began to negotiate. Finally, I agreed to let the major put his gun in the trunk; he could get it out if we faced any real danger.

There is always an element of fear for a journalist covering a war, but a good reporter is usually so busy trying to find a story that he doesn't think about it. The risk of death or injury for reporters is one of chance, maybe a bit higher than getting hit by a bus in New York, but still fairly low. However, having a soldier with a gun in my car could only increase the odds that someone might start shooting at it.

The second of what would become a day of disagreements came as we approached Gaza. The major wanted to get his rifle out of the trunk. I argued that I had driven through Gaza without incident for the previous two days. Again, we reached an impasse. Again, we compromised. He agreed to keep the rifle in the trunk if we drove the long way around Gaza. That made us even later reaching the Sinai road at El Arish.

Once in the Sinai, it became clear that Major Shlomo was going to be a major headache. We had gone less than a third of the way toward the canal when he told me we had gone far enough. We quarreled as I continued to drive.

"We can't go any farther," the major said.

"Nonsense," I replied with what I thought was an irrefutable argument. "I went almost all the way to the canal yesterday. Nobody stopped me."

"I don't know about that," he said. "But I have my orders. There's a medical unit just ahead. We can stop there, and you can conduct some interviews."

Interviews are a poor second cousin to firsthand accounts of a battle, especially for someone like me, who is basically shy and has never gotten used to going up to strangers and asking them questions they didn't want to answer. But I thought it would not be time wasted to talk to some of the soldiers just back from the front. I wandered around, taking notes while the photographer went off to snap pictures.

I saw one soldier sitting on the ground by a jeep and went over to talk to him. He gave me his name, but I knew I could only refer to him as Corporal Yigal. The corporal said he was a senior in college and he resented being in the desert risking his life when he should be studying. He had been with a tank that had taken a hit, and he had come back with one of the crew who had been wounded. I asked him how the battle was going.

"It's going nowhere," he said. "We move forward a couple hundred yards, then we pull back a couple hundred yards. It's like we're playing tag and we take turns being 'it.' It's crazy. Kids are dying out there, and for what? A stretch of desert? Why don't we just give it back to them? Israel doesn't need it."

The fighting in the Sinai was mainly a tank battle, with Israeli and Egyptian tanks chasing one another across the desert.

I asked him what morale was like.

"Well," he said. "Nobody's laughing and joking about spending the weekend in Cairo anymore."

Corporal Yigal seemed impressed with my being a journalist.

"You reporters must be really brave," he said. "You come all the way out to the desert and go looking for a battle. And you don't even have a gun."

I thought I should set him straight. "We're not brave, Corporal. For one thing, we can stay as far away from the fighting as we want. And if it gets too hot, I can always get in my car and drive back to Tel Aviv. I can run away anytime I want. You can't."

I was ready to get back in the car and drive farther west when Major Shlomo came up and suggested we head back to Tel Aviv. I was astonished. I pointed out that it was still early in the day and that I needed to find some action.

The major insisted that we had to leave so we could get back to Tel Aviv before dark and that it wasn't safe to drive farther west. I countered that it didn't matter whether we returned before dark or not and that we hadn't come to the Sinai for our safety. To my surprise, the U.P.I. photographer agreed with the major. I gave in, and we drove back.

As soon as I got to the bureau, I told Tom I didn't want to travel with an army officer or anyone else in the future. I didn't need to spell it out for Tom, and he agreed.

The days were beginning to take on a certain routine. Just like millions of other people around the world, I would arise just before dawn, hurriedly get dressed, rush out to my car, and listen to the news on the radio as I drove to work. The only difference with my commute was that I was driving to the desert to cover a war.

The next day, I stopped again at the kibbutz shop for a cup of coffee. Sarah, the American girl from Chicago, was there. I asked her how things were on the kibbutz.

"It's starting to get really tense," she said. "Everybody thought the war would be over in a week and the men would come back to help with the harvest."

"I don't think the war will be over today," I said.

"No," she said. "Everybody is on edge. The Russian men are really upset. Some of them are talking about how they should go back to the Soviet Union."

One of the big political issues of that time was whether the Soviet Union would allow Russian Jews to emigrate to Israel. Many applied for permission, but the Kremlin authorities would allow only a certain number to leave each year. Those who were denied permission to leave were called *refuseniks*. One of the reasons the Soviets gave for their refusal was that the émigrés might end up working against Soviet interests, which included the Arab countries. As an incentive to increase the number of Russian Jews allowed in Israel, the immigrants were exempt from military service.

"The situation is getting worse every day," Sarah said. "They are really angry at having to work double shifts in the fields to get the harvest in because all the other men have gone off to fight."

"Would any of them talk to me?" I asked, smelling a story.

"I doubt it," Sarah said. "The Russians stay completely apart from everybody else. They even eat at separate tables, and they won't talk to the Americans."

Still, I made a mental note to take some extra time one day to go to the kibbutz and do a story. I got another cup of coffee to go and drove on toward the Sinai.

The northern Sinai road was as busy as ever. All along the way, the desert was dotted with the small makeshift Sukkoth tabernacles that soldiers had built. I drove almost to the point where I had seen the tank battle two days earlier when I saw what looked like a tour bus ahead of me. I couldn't imagine that Israel had already started organizing guided tours of Sinai battlefields, but I stopped to investigate.

As it turned out, the bus was a sort of mobile field headquarters for the top Israeli command in the Sinai. Several other reporters were there, and we were told that there would be a press briefing on the bus. We all climbed aboard.

Brigadier General Kalman Magen, the commander of the Israeli southern front, arrived by jeep a few minutes later. General Magen said the Egyptians were marshaling their forces along the Sinai side of the canal for what appeared to be a major breakthrough attempt, pouring men, armor, and artillery across the Suez Canal.

In one very candid assessment, the general said that Israeli warplanes were attacking the Egyptian bridges across the canal in an effort to halt the flow of men and arms into the Sinai, but that the Egyptian engineers repaired them within hours.

"We destroy in the day, and they repair at night," he said. "Destroy and repair. Destroy and repair. It's like children's toys. You can tear it apart, and in a few hours it's back, fixed again."

General Magen said the Egyptians had started their offensive to break out of the front the previous day with human-wave attacks but that they had been repulsed.

"It started with artillery shelling," the general said, describing the Egyptian attack. "Then they attacked in waves. And even with casualties, they pushed again and again."

Remembering the bridge-building machine I saw earlier, I was about to ask about Israel's own plans for crossing the canal, but a barrage of artillery suddenly boomed outside, and an air-raid siren screamed from somewhere. The press conference was over. We all rushed off the bus. Soldiers were scurrying everywhere, and we all searched the sky for Egyptian planes. None were to be seen.

But the big news that day was not in what an Israeli general said in the desert. Iraq announced it was sending a volunteer force to fight on the side of Syria. It was not good news, not because the Iraqi army itself posed any great threat, but because it might prompt Jordan or even the Soviet Union to join the war as well. The unspoken fear was that if either of the two superpowers—the United States or the Soviet Union—became directly involved, the conflict could escalate into a world war.

THE YOM KIPPUR WAR

An Israeli tank crew driving past a knocked-out Syrian tank on the Golan Heights on the third day of the war

At left: An Egyptian MiG warplane
streaking across the sky on an attack
of Israeli positions in the Sinai

Below: Israeli artillery forces pounded
Syrian positions in a nonstop bombardment with long-range 155-millimeter
guns that filled the air with smoke and
deafening noise.

A Jordanian tank arriving on the Golan Heights to support Syria in the closing days of the war

Israeli soldiers marching along the northern Sinai road to reinforce positions against Egyptian forces as cease-fire talks to end the war were under way

The wreckage of Soviet-built T-62 Syrian tanks littered the landscape of the Golan Heights as Israeli tanks gained the upper hand in the fighting.

Jerusalem is considered a holy city by all three Western religions. The Western Wall, a sacred site to Jews, is in the shadow of the Dome of the Rock, one of Islam's holiest shrines.

CHAPTER 9

THE QUIET FRONT

THROUGHOUT THE FIRST WEEK of the war, the focus had been on the northern and southern fronts in the Golan and Sinai. With the entry of Iraq into the war and the possibility that Jordan might enter the fighting, Tom asked me to drive over to Jerusalem and then go north up along the Israeli border with Jordan to do a story on the "quiet front."

Known throughout the world as the Holy City, Jerusalem is held sacred by all three Western religions—Judaism, Christianity, and Islam. It was settled by 4000 B.C. and was first captured by King David from the Canaanites in 1000 B.C. Jews have regarded it as their spiritual capital since Solomon built the First Temple there.

Over the centuries, the city fell to many conquerors—Babylon, Rome, the Muslims, the crusaders, the Muslims again. From the creation of Israel until 1967, the city was divided into East and West Jerusalem. East Jerusalem, known as the Old City, belonged to Jordan; West Jerusalem, the newer part of the city, was Israeli. In 1967, Israel captured East Jerusalem and now claimed the entire city as its capital.

There was much I would have liked to see in Jerusalem: the Church of the Holy Sepulchre, a major Christian site; the Dome of the Rock, which is one of the holiest mosques to Muslims; and the Western Wall, also known as the Wailing Wall, the only remaining part of the Second Temple, which was destroyed by the Roman emperor Titus in A.D. 70, and is a sacred place for Jews. But my story was elsewhere that day.

The drive up the Jordan River valley provided a stark contrast to the drive across the Sinai. If the desert road had been choked with the traffic of war, the highway north of Jerusalem was deserted. After driving several miles, I saw what appeared to be a military outpost in the distance. I stopped the car and looked through my binoculars. I could see an Israeli Star of David flag flying over the main building and a few soldiers standing outside. As I gazed through the binoculars, it seemed that one of the soldiers was looking back at me through his own field glasses. I decided to take a few pictures. This story on the quiet front was turning out to be a nonstory, but I thought I might as well get a snapshot to go with it.

Looking through the camera lens, I saw a small cloud of dust moving along the dirt road that ran between the outpost and the highway. As it got closer, I could see that the jeep was speeding like a fire engine racing to a three-alarm blaze. The jeep's tires squealed as it pulled onto the highway and screeched to a halt behind my car.

Two Israeli soldiers got out, Uzi automatic rifles under their arms. One demanded to know what I was doing there. The other asked to see my credentials.

As a journalist based in Rome, I had a press card issued by the Italian Foreign Ministry and another by the Holy See, the Vatican government, which is a sovereign nation in the heart of Rome. It was the latter I pulled out of my wallet to show the soldiers, trying to convince them that I normally covered the Roman Catholic Church.

They weren't buying it. And they weren't answering any questions. One returned to the jeep and got on a phone, presumably to consult with someone back at the outpost. They seemed to be debating whether to arrest me.

After a few moments, he came back to where I was standing in the middle of the road by my car. He then asked to see my camera.

"What were you taking pictures of?" he asked.

"Just the empty terrain around here," I replied, truthfully enough.

"This is a restricted area," he said. "You can't take pictures of military areas."

"I've been taking pictures all week in the Sinai, and nobody has tried to stop me," I replied, also truthfully enough, but without mentioning that some of the pictures I took had been censored.

"Well, you can't take pictures here," he said, and proceeded to open the back of my camera, pull out the roll of film, and pocket it.

"You can go," he said, handing me back my press card. "But you'll have to leave this area. No civilian personnel are allowed. And you can't take any pictures."

It didn't seem to be a good time for a freedom-of-the-press speech, and by this point I was feeling fortunate that I wasn't speeding back to the outpost in their jeep.

When I got back to the U.P.I. bureau in Tel Aviv, there was a buzz of activity. Tuohy and David Harris, a reporter for the Hearst newspapers, had just arrived and were recounting how four Iraqi soldiers had surrendered to them on the Golan Heights.

Tuohy and Harris had been driving around when they came upon a patrol of soldiers. They first thought the soldiers, in full battle gear, were Syrians. They were going to make a quick U-turn, but the soldiers waved them down to stop. The soldiers turned out to be part of the contingent of volunteers that Iraq had sent to join the war and had become separated, either by accident or desertion, from their unit.

None of the soldiers spoke much English, but it became clear that they wanted to surrender and were asking Tuohy and Harris to take them to the Israeli headquarters. They clearly had no desire to be in Israel fighting a war. One Iraqi offered Tuohy his gun, then his helmet, if he would drive them to an Israeli camp so they could surrender.

Just as Tuohy and Harris were winding up their story, Mitch Vinocur showed up. Mitch, a young U.P.I. reporter from the Brussels bureau, had been in the Golan all day. He was at an Israeli bunker near the front when a sudden Syrian artillery attack came.

The Israelis had made a dramatic turnaround on the Golan, and after a week of heavy fighting, they stood poised to break through the Syrian lines. As Mitch hunkered down with the Israeli soldiers to weather the Syrian attack, a jeep drove up, and its passengers jumped out and joined them in the bunker. One of them was immediately recognizable by his trademark eye patch. It was Moshe Dayan.

While the attack ended, Mitch followed the defense minister outside and got a brief interview that provided one of the famous lines from the war.

"The Syrians will learn," Dayan told Mitch, "that the road from Damascus to Tel Aviv also leads from Tel Aviv to Damascus."

But the most important news that night did not involve Iraqi

soldiers surrendering to American reporters or even the Israeli army reaching the gates of Damascus. It was a story that turned the tide of the war, but at the time it happened, we couldn't report it.

Israeli forces continued to hammer at Syrian positions on the Golan Heights with heavy artillery guns.

Real war is not like the movies or computer games, where neither side ever seems to run out of bullets or tanks or planes. The Israelis lost a large number of weapons and used up a lot of ammunition in the first twenty-four hours of the war, and they had been appealing to Washington for arms reinforcements almost since the opening shots.

If the start of the war had caught Israel by surprise, it was no less of a shock to the leaders in the United States and the Soviet

Union, and the initial Arab successes had stunned both Washington and Moscow. Although he was preoccupied with the Vietnam War and the Watergate scandal, President Nixon knew what was at risk in the Middle East. He told his secretary of state, Henry Kissinger, that Israel must not be allowed to lose.

With Israel reeling from the first Arab attacks, Prime Minister Golda Meir asked the United States for help. Kissinger later recalled that he was woken up three times in the night by the Israeli ambassador asking America to send arms. The third time, Kissinger said he would take the matter up with the president the next day. In Kissinger's account, the ambassador replied that Mrs. Meir had told him, "Tomorrow may be too late."

The United States first started resupplying Israel using El Al planes to carry arms from American bases in Europe. However, these flights could not bring the heavy armor reinforcements that Israel felt it needed. By the end of that first week of the war, Nixon made the decision to use giant American military transport planes that were based in Europe to send whatever arms Israel needed.

That airlift began the next day. The Israeli censors, however, blocked any report of the U.S. military planes landing in Israel. Even television reports were censored. The Israelis delayed transmissions for a few seconds before they were beamed back to the United States and would cut them off if they objected to anything in the report. In the end, it was a TV reporter who finally got the news out about the American airlift.

During his broadcast, the TV correspondent observed that "the night is full of stars here in Tel Aviv." Even the censor saw nothing wrong with a bit of weather reporting. However, by previous agreement with his editors in New York, the television reporter was delivering a coded message that the night sky was full of American planes, each of which had the big blue star that was the symbol of the U.S. Air Force on its tail.

Two days after the United States began its airlift, the same pontoon bridge–building machine I had seen on my first day in the Sinai spanned the Suez Canal just north of Bitter Lake. It provided a gateway to Israelis crossing into Egypt for the first time since Moses led the Jews out of bondage in biblical times.

The war dragged on for another two weeks. But as the fighting reached a sort of stalemate, U.P.I. reduced the number of reporters covering the war, and I returned to Rome a few days before a United Nations cease-fire formally went into effect on October 22. Skirmishing continued for days afterward, however, as each side jockeyed for better positions, and at one point it appeared that the cease-fire might collapse altogether. It was not until the early morning hours of Sunday, October 28, that Egyptian and Israeli generals met in a tent on a desert road between Suez and Cairo and finally made peace with a handshake. It was the first time the two countries had held direct negotiations, and it marked the last time Egypt and Israel fought on a battlefield.

In the end, both Israel and Egypt could claim a victory of sorts. By the time the guns fell silent, Israel held more territory than it had at the beginning of the war, and its soldiers were on Egyptian soil. But Egyptian forces also were still camped in the Sinai, in territory that had been under Israeli control when the war began. Syria, on the other hand, had seen its army, after delivering a stunning blow on the first day, driven back and Israeli forces within artillery range of Damascus.

For Egypt, the war was also a tremendous psychological success

Israeli and Egyptian commanders met in a tent to sign a cease-fire that marked the end of the 1973 Middle East war.

that erased the disgrace of its humiliating loss six years earlier. For Israel, despite a disorganized start, its soldiers had overcome the greatest threat the Jewish state had faced since its inception.

At the end of the 1973 war, as blue-helmeted United Nations peacekeepers entered the no-man's-land between the Egyptian and Israeli lines in the Sinai to separate the warring armies, soldiers from both sides rose up and stared at one another. The Egyptians reacted first. They left their firing positions and walked toward the Israelis. A nervous Israeli company commander didn't know what to do and radioed for instructions.

"Take them prisoner," he was told.

"They don't want to surrender," the Israeli informed head-quarters. "They want to shake hands."

The 1973 Middle East war was the last full-scale war between Israel and its Arab neighbors. But it was not the end of warfare. For the next three decades and beyond, the Israelis and the Palestinians continued to fight what had become a sort of Fifty Years War and counting. As the twenty-first century began, they seemed to be no closer to a solution of how to live together than they had been at the creation of Israel in 1948. Leaders on both sides still seemed more inclined to shake their fists rather than shake hands. Like so many things in the desert, peace still seemed like just another mirage.

After the 1973 war, Egypt forged a new alliance with the United States, sealed with a visit by President Nixon in which he was greeted by large crowds in Alexandria (above) and Cairo.

CHAPTER 10

WAR AND PEACE

THE AFTERMATH of the 1973 war brought many political changes in the Middle East. One of the biggest came the following year, when President Sadat broke with the Soviet Union and ordered all Soviet advisers to leave Egypt. Egypt had been allied with Moscow since the 1950s, and the fact that Sadat was now turning to the United States was a major shift in the balance of power, not only in the Middle East but in the Cold War.

The change in alliances was formally sealed with a state visit by President Nixon to Egypt. It was the last big story I personally covered in the Middle East. It was always a joy for me to return to Egypt. I loved Cairo and the Egyptians, whom I always found warm and welcoming, and this time the Egyptian capital was in a mood of celebration.

Nixon traveled to the ancient city of Alexandria, which had been founded by Alexander the Great in 332 B.C., then to Cairo. Everywhere he went, Nixon drew large crowds. It was astonishing to me to see American and Egyptian flags at street corners and to hear Egyptian taxi drivers, waiters, and ordinary Cairenes in coffee bars heralding the new friendship between the United States and

Egypt. If Sadat's political moves toward the West were viewed with suspicion by the rest of the Arab world, they clearly had the support of most of the Egyptians. By the time the American president reached Cairo, he was cheered like a rock star at a concert.

The following year I returned to New York, and for the rest of my journalistic career, my involvement in the Middle East story was from an editor's desk, first at U.P.I.'s world headquarters in New York and later at *The New York Times*. It was the one story that would not go away. Every week, it seemed there was some big headline from the Middle East—another Palestinian guerrilla attack or hijacking, or the news that the Israelis were building another settlement on land the Palestinians regarded as theirs.

Only occasionally over the years did the headlines report moves for peace. One of the boldest attempts at peace came four years after the guns fell silent in the Sinai, and once again it was Egypt who first offered to shake hands.

In a speech to the Egyptian Parliament in 1977, President Sadat said he was "prepared to go to the ends of the earth" to talk peace for the Middle East. Ten days later, Sadat was invited by the new Israeli prime minister, Menachem Begin, to Jersualem to address the Israeli Parliament. If this was not a journey literally to the ends of the earth, it certainly was so figuratively. In his speech to the Israeli Parliament, Sadat declared, "No more war."

President Jimmy Carter invited both sides to the American presidential retreat at Camp David. After two years of negotiations by their envoys, President Sadat and Prime Minister Begin signed a peace treaty in Washington in 1978 that became known as the Camp David Accords. Under its terms, Israel would give the Sinai back to Egypt and the two countries would establish diplomatic relations. The treaty also pledged that the two sides would begin negotiating for Palestinian autonomy in the West Bank and Gaza.

The treaty virtually guaranteed there would not be another full-scale Middle East war, since none of the other Arab countries would go to war against Israel without Egypt. But Arafat and the P.L.O. rejected it outright, and Egypt became ostracized by other Arab countries, some of whom recalled their ambassadors and broke relations with Cairo.

In the end, Sadat paid for his peace attempts with his life. Two years after signing the treaty with Israel, Sadat was assassinated in Cairo by an Islamic militant as he reviewed a military parade.

The turmoil that followed the 1973 war brought changes in Israel as well. Although Mrs. Meir won reelection as prime minister just two months after the war ended, the Labor Party lost the next elections, in 1977, to the new right-wing Likud Party. Menachem Begin became prime minister, and Ariel Sharon was given a cabinet position.

One of the greatest tragedies that evolved out of both the 1970 civil war in Jordan and the 1973 Arab-Israeli war resulted in the virtual destruction of Lebanon in a civil war and included a shocking Israeli involvement in a massacre of Palestinians.

At the time of Lebanon's independence from France in 1945, a formula was set up to provide the Christians, who were then in the majority, and the Muslims a proportionate share of power. But thirty years later, the Muslims, whose population had increased because of the tens of thousands of Palestinians who fled there after the civil war in Jordan, had become a majority, and they wanted a greater voice in the government to reflect their increased numbers.

When fighting broke out in Lebanon, a plethora of private armies sprang up. There were the Phalangists, who were Christian;

Anwar el-Sadat of Egypt made an overture for peace.

Menachem Begin invited Sadat to Jerusalem.

Ariel Sharon later became prime minister of Israel.

the Lebanese National Movement, which was made up of Sunni Muslims and Palestinians; the South Lebanese Army, who were Christians in southern Lebanon; Hezbollah, a Shiite Muslim group; and the Druze, an independent sect that is an offshoot of Islam. To top it off, Syria sent its troops into Lebanon to seize territory that it believed had belonged to Syria in the first place.

The P.L.O. guerrillas in southern Lebanon began to stage attacks against Israel. Several times, Israel sent troops into south Lebanon to halt the attacks. Each time, the attacks would stop for a while, then begin again. In 1982, Israel decided it had to act more decisively and invaded Lebanon, eventually occupying Beirut. The Israeli action forced the P.L.O. to leave Lebanon for Tunisia. But it also led to one of the biggest blots in Israel's history.

In September that year, the Phalangists wanted revenge on the Palestinians for the assassination of one of their leaders. With the knowledge and approval of Sharon, who by this time was the Israeli defense minister, and as Israeli army troops stood guard outside, Phalangist fighters entered two Palestinian refugee camps in Beirut and over the course of two days and nights killed up to 1,000 Palestinians, including old people, women, and children.

When news of the massacre reached the outside world, there was stunned outrage. At first, Sharon tried to deny Israeli involvement. But an Israeli commission investigating it found that Sharon bore "personal responsibility" for the massacre, and he was forced out as defense minister. A year later, Begin himself resigned as prime minister.

Shortly after the massacre, President Ronald Reagan ordered U.S. Marines to Lebanon to try to stop the civil war. They stayed just over a year, suffering a suicide bombing attack on their head-

The bodies of victims lay on the streets of the Sabra and Shatila refugee camps in Beirut following the massacre of Palestinians by Lebanese Christian militias while Israeli forces stood guard outside.

quarters at the Beirut airport that killed 241 American servicemen, before Reagan ordered them home.

The decade of the 1990s started with another war. It began in August when Iraq invaded and overran Kuwait, a small country on the Persian Gulf, and threatened Saudi Arabia, an American ally and the source of much of the world's oil. President George H. Bush first went to the United Nations to condemn the Iraqi action, then carefully built a coalition of other Arab nations, but not Israel, to join together to drive the Iraqis out of Kuwait.

For the first time, American and Arab soldiers fought alongside one another in a war against another Arab country, and, by extension, in defense of Israel. The Israelis appeared content to sit on the sidelines, although there was an anxious period when Iraq began firing Scud missiles at Israel. The fear was that if Israel retaliated, it would be hard to keep the American-Arab coalition together.

The Israelis, however, remained firm in their pledge not to get involved, and the American-Arab armies drove the Iraqis out of Kuwait, all the way to the outskirts of Baghdad, the Iraqi capital. The agreement ending the war, however, left Saddam Hussein, the Iraqi leader, in power, a fact that would have devastating results a decade later.

Perhaps the brightest chance for peace in the Middle East came in 1993, and it took the world by surprise. It was suddenly announced in August that Israel and the P.L.O. had been holding secret talks in Oslo, Norway, for months and had agreed to a Declaration of Principles, under which the Palestinians would formally recognize Israel and the Israelis would turn over parts of the West Bank and the Gaza Strip to Palestinian control.

It was signed by Yitzhak Rabin, the Israeli prime minister, and P.L.O. leader Yasir Arafat at the White House. With the new American president, Bill Clinton, looking on, Arafat and Rabin shook hands. A year later, Jordan and Israel signed a peace treaty.

The hope of peace that came with the signing of the Oslo agreements was again shattered by an assassin's bullet. This time, an ultra-Orthodox Jew who opposed Israel's pact with the Palestinians shot and killed Rabin at a peace rally in Jerusalem.

With the dawn of the new century, the mood on each side was one of bitterness and mistrust, and two old warriors who had never believed in compromise were in charge: Ariel Sharon was elected prime minister of Israel, and Arafat, who had moved back to the occupied territories as part of the Oslo Accords, still led the P.L.O.

An attempt by President Clinton to revive the Middle East peace process during the last year of his presidency failed when Arafat walked out of the talks.

President Anwar el-Sadat of Egypt and Prime Minister Menachem Begin of Israel signed a peace agreement brokered by President Jimmy Carter in 1979.

Prime Minister Yitzhak Rabin of Israel and Yasir Arafat, the P.L.O. leader, shaking hands on another peace accord in 1993 while President Bill Clinton looks on

Sharon encouraged the building of new Israeli settlements in areas that were destined to be turned over to the Palestinians, including Gaza. Radical Palestinians launched a new uprising and expanded use of suicide bombers to attack Israelis. In response, Sharon instructed Israeli soldiers to shoot to kill any guerrilla suspects and to destroy Palestinian houses suspected of harboring guerrillas.

When the Israeli reprisals did not stop the Palestinian bombers, Sharon decided to isolate Israel. He began building a wall between Israel and the parts of the West Bank occupied by Palestinians and ordered Israel's withdrawal from its settlements in Gaza.

A new Palestinian uprising that included suicide bombing attacks prompted Israel to build a wall along parts of the West Bank.

It was easy for each side to justify its actions. Israeli civilians could not live in perpetual fear that every time they boarded a bus or went to buy groceries they risked being killed by a suicide bomber. And Palestinians could not be expected to sit idly by while Israeli troops bulldozed their homes and sprayed their streets with gunfire.

With the use of suicide bombers, terror became a weapon in itself. Civilians rather than soldiers now became the main targets, and the spread of terrorist attacks around the world threatened to create a virtual state of endless war.

On September 11, 2001, militant Muslim terrorists crashed hjacked planes into the Twin Towers in New York City and the Pentagon in Washington, D.C., killing more than 3,000 people. While the attacks on the United States were not directly related to the Arab-Israeli conflict, they had ominous ramifications for the Middle East as a region. The attacks led President George W. Bush to declare a "war on terror." U.S. forces promptly invaded Afghanistan and drove its Taliban government from power. The Taliban had harbored a terrorist group called Al Qaeda that had plotted the September 11th attacks. A few months later, Bush ordered an invasion of Iraq, although that country had no part in the attacks on America, and overthrew the regime of Saddam Hussein. The American military action stirred old hatreds among Muslims, Christians, and Jews and produced uncertain consequences not only for the Middle East, but for the rest of the world as well.

There once was hope that a new generation of leaders on both sides would find the way to peace. Yasir Arafat died in 2004, and a moderate Palestinian named Mahmoud Abbas took over as leader

In 2006, Palestinian voters elected a radical group known as Hamas, which had supported the violent uprising, to replace the P.L.O. as its government.

of the P.L.O. But he had little success in halting attacks on Israel by militant guerrilla groups like Hamas, a Muslim group that had carried out suicide bombing attacks in Israel. A little over a year later, Ariel Sharon suffered a disabling stroke and was succeeded as Israeli prime minister by Ehud Olmert, who only months earlier had helped Sharon establish a new political party called Kadima.

In January 2006, Palestinian voters overwhelmingly elected the radical group Hamas to replace the P.L.O. as their government. An ensuing power struggle between the factions led to open fighting that brought Palestinians to the brink of civil war. The dispute ended in an arrangement that left the P.L.O. in charge on the West Bank and Hamas in control of the Gaza Strip. In the midst of the Palestinian political turmoil, the capture of two Israeli soldiers by Hezbollah, a Shiite Muslim faction, triggered a month-long war. Israel sent 10,000 troops into Lebanon, but failed to defeat Hezbollah, and another U.N. peacekeeping force was sent to enforce a ceasefire.

The ascension of Hamas, which both Israel and the United States listed as a terrorist organization, prompted Israel in 2007 to impose a blockade of Gaza, virtually paralyzing the territory's economy and limiting the flow of food, medicines, and other supplies to Palestinians living there. An Israeli raid into Gaza in November 2008 prompted Hamas to renounce a cease-fire and launch a steady barrage of rocket fire into Israel, and that led to an armed Israeli incursion into the territory just before the end of the year.

The ferocity of the Israeli assault was staggering. Many people who might have been sympathetic to a country retaliating against rocket attacks on its citizens were appalled at the scope of killing and destruction Israeli soldiers unleashed on the Palestinians in Gaza. More than 1,300 Palestinians were killed in Israel's three-week campaign in Gaza, nearly half of them women and children.

Another questionable factor in the Israeli military action was its timing. The United States had just elected a new president, Barack Obama, who advocated talks with all parties in the Middle East. Some analysts believed Israel wanted to carry out its Gaza offensive before he took office on January 20, 2009. Israel itself was getting ready for elections, and the mixed feelings many Israelis had about Gaza figured in the political campaign. In the end, Benjamin Netanyahu and his Likud party held a narrow lead in the voting and he was named the new Israeli prime minister. Because his margin of victory was so small, Netanyahu was forced to form a coalition government with his Labor Party rivals and promise to work for peace with the Palestinians.

President Obama quickly made it clear that the Middle East would be a major item on his foreign policy agenda. He sent his new Secretary of State, Hillary Clinton, to the region and appointed George J. Mitchell as a special envoy. Still, the anger brought on by the Israeli action in Gaza only deepened the hard feelings on both sides and the threat of renewed fighting clouded the new president's peace overtures.

But even the most bitter of wars end, and people who were once enemies can, in time, become neighbors. Only in the Middle East does it seem as though there is no end in sight.

As I look back over the decades, I often wonder what the world will be like a hundred years from now. Will the Middle East conflict finally become only a chapter in a history book? Or will the fighting and killing still be going on?

ACKNOWLEDGMENTS

First of all, I would like to acknowledge the many journalists who have covered the Middle East conflict over the decades with far more tenacity and perspicacity than I, and from whom I have learned much. I would like to thank Cynthia Platt for her initial support for the book, and Joan Powers for her editorial guidance throughout its writing. Sherry Fatla provided her usual expertise in its design, and Kaylan Adair contributed helpful research assistance. I would also like to thank Mattie Kahn for reading the book in its early stages and offering valuable suggestions. I am happily indebted to the Bogliasco Foundation's Liguria Study Center, where much of the book was written, for its hospitality and for providing a place for uninterrupted work. Finally, as in all my endeavors, I am grateful for the support of my wife, LuAnn Walther.

Rabinovich, Abraham. *The Yom Kippur War: The Epic Encounter That Transformed the Middle East.* New York: Schocken Books, 2004.

Herzog, Chaim. Updated by Shlomo Gazit. *The Arab-Israeli Wars: War and Peace in the Middle East.* New York: Vintage Books, 2005.

Friedman, Thomas L. *From Beirut to Jerusalem.* New York: Anchor Books, 1990.

Boyne, Walter J. *The Yom Kippur War: And the Airlift That Saved Israel.* New York: Thomas Dunne Books/St. Martin's Griffin, 2003.

PHOTOGRAPHY CREDITS

Page numbers in *italic* type indicate illustrations.

AN UNFORGETTABLE MOMENT IN HISTORY

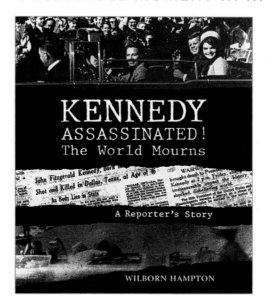

Kennedy Assassinated!
The World Mourns: A Reporter's Story
Wilborn Hampton

★ "Terrific. . . . Hampton was a novice reporter at U.P.I. in Dallas on the day President Kennedy was assassinated. . . . He is at his best as he describes himself in the midst of the fevered activity . . . all the while maintaining a journalistic distance as he reports events. . . . This book brings those days home to a younger generation." —*Booklist* (starred review)

Hardcover ISBN 978-1-56402-811-2

www.candlewick.com

A DAY THAT CHANGED THE WORLD

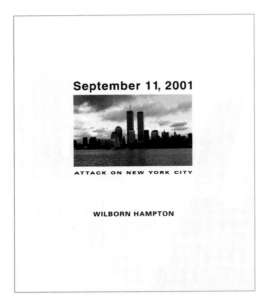

September 11, 2001:
Attack on New York City
Wilborn Hampton

★ "Hampton presents a personal, emotional account of the attack on the World
Trade Center, profiling two people who were in the towers when the planes
hit, the family of a woman who perished, and some who helped with the
rescue effort, including members of the NYFD's Ladder Company 6. . . .
Strong reporting." —*Publishers Weekly* (starred review)

Hardcover ISBN 978-0-7636-1949-7
Paperback ISBN 978-0-7636-3635-7

www.candlewick.com